The
Hourglass
Solution

The
Hourglass
Solution

A Boomer's Guide to
the Rest of Your Life

Jeff Johnson, PhD
and
Paula Forman, PhD

Da Capo
LIFE
LONG

A Member of the Perseus Books Group

Set in 11.5-point point Adobe Garamond by the Perseus Books Group

Cataloging-in-Publication data for this book is available from the Library of Congress.

First Da Capo Press edition 2009
ISBN: 978-0-7382-1246-3

Published by Da Capo Press
A Member of the Perseus Books Group
www.dacapopress.com

Da Capo Press books are available at special discounts for bulk purchases in the U.S. by corporations, institutions, and other organizations. For more information, please contact the Special Markets Department at the Perseus Books Group, 2300 Chestnut Street, Suite 200, Philadelphia, PA, 19103, or call (800) 810-4145, ext. 5000, or e-mail special.markets@perseusbooks.com.

10 9 8 7 6 5 4 3 2 1

To Hy, always.
—*Jeff*

To Philip, Izzy, Jon, and Owen—and
my folks, Roz and Ben.
—*Paula*

Slaves got options.

Options, you dig?

I'm talkin' escape . . .

Revolt . . .

Death.

Options.

But cowards ain't got shit!

Cowards only have . . .

Consequences.

Dig me, do you dig me.

—STEW AND HEIDI RODEWALD,
Passing Strange

Note

All of the people discussed in this book are real and their stories are true. Nearly all of the names and most of the identifying details have been changed to protect individual identities.

Contents

Introduction

Our journey began at an idyllic, day-long party in the country. We hadn't seen each other in a long time when we met up at our friends' birthday party—Matthew was turning forty and Douglas was fifty. It was a glorious event in every visible way: friends and relatives from three continents, lots of kids, and a few very excited dogs. Even the weather cooperated. A beautiful early summer afternoon near Coxsackie, New York, as far from civilization and the demands of everyday life as one could get in a single afternoon.

We knew most of the guests, but there were many who seemed different from the way we remembered them. What used to look like confidence, now felt like bravado. The faces of the former ingenues were older and etched with a trace of bitterness. Some golden couples were a little less golden. The two of us got to talking.

Jeff: I had moved three times since Paula and I had last spoken. I had just left my job as CEO of an advertising agency in Atlanta and was taking a breather after a difficult couple of years. I was happy to be back in New York, but a bit anxious about the next step. My partner was writing for a long-running TV series, so I wasn't as worried about money as I usually am. I just felt uneasy and very unsettled.

Paula: I had left advertising, too. I had been president of Wells Rich Greene/BDDP and had recently switched gears. I was teaching sociology at Hunter College in New York City. It was the hardest work I had ever done—four performances a week to a packed house. Anyone who has done it knows what I mean. But it is lonely work, and I was missing the collaborative environment of advertising. My husband, Philip, was traveling more than usual; the kids were grown and on their way. I had a lot of freedom, but just like Jeff, I felt uneasy.

Jeff: We were both at a transition point. Neither one of us was truly unhappy. Nor was there any crisis—no divorce, no major health issues—just a feeling that something wasn't right.

Paula: We would wander off to chat with others at the party, but after a quick review of "What have you been doing for the last five years?" it was rough going. Some friends were subdued, some a little frenetic, and some just sad. We kept coming back to each other because it seemed as though our conversation wasn't finished.

Jeff: As it happened, that took several years.

What began as a conversation about life transitions and turning points became an exploration that would engage us both for some time to come.

On one level, life was very good for both of us. We were healthy, happy with our partners, and past the grinding competition that had characterized our work lives a decade before. We weren't rich, but weren't hurting, either. Many of the people we knew were similarly blessed, but middle age was hitting us all pretty hard in a way that wasn't easy to describe. Something was happening, and we didn't think it was "just a midlife crisis."

A midlife crisis, we knew from experience, typically hits sometime between forty and forty-five. We remembered when that was going around—dramatic self-doubt and the "is that all there is?" blues. Halfway through your life, you wondered where it went. A midlife crisis was about the past, and the obvious answer was "get over it"—move on. Most people did.

What we were feeling and observing in our peers was not the same as a midlife crisis. This phenomenon was sometimes expressed as panic, but more often it was an unnameable anxiety. The big difference was that it wasn't about the past or regret about youth that had come and gone all too fast. What we ourselves were feeling and noticing in the people around us was definitively *not* about the past. It was about the future.

> **Paula:** We had grown up in an era of unprecedented opportunity and personal freedom. The freedom to make fundamental choices about life was a universal baby boomer expectation that we had eagerly embraced. Some of the choices were good and some not so good, but our generation was indelibly marked by the sense that a life of our own choosing was our prerogative.
>
> **Jeff:** But we had arrived at a point where there appeared to be no more options. Choices we

made decades earlier were no longer exciting. With the loss of excitement came a loss of vitality. In spite of their many successes in the world, our friends and associates seemed uncharacteristically confused about what the next life stage might look like.

Paula: For those nearing fifty, wry humor and some denial took the place of planning. For those who had sixty in their sights, anxiety was overwhelming. People who had always been adventurers, ever armed with good humor and fresh ideas, were retreating—and it was scary.

Sharp insights about human behavior were our bread and butter in the advertising business. We had paid the bills with our ability to spot trends before they became mainstream. Our most valuable skill was listening. As "killer listeners," we were hearing something quite perplexing among our friends and in the population at large. We were hearing insecurity from people who had every reason to feel certain. We needed to find out if this problem was idiosyncratic to our small group or if we had uncovered something bigger.

Once a grad student, always a grad student: We hit the stacks and plumbed the literature about midlife. Much has been written about boomers at all life stages, and there are self-help books for every aspect of life transition: saving for retirement, exercising away your spare tire, turning your hobby into a part-time job. That's not what we were looking for. So we kept digging.

The statistical data, it turned out, held some real surprises. The morbidity of boomers in their fifties was showing some very odd blips: growing rates of reported suicide and a surprisingly high incidence of "accidental death" for this age group. Reported depression for those in midlife, both treated and nontreated, was reaching unprecedented levels, and these symptoms cut across all social classes.

Jeff: We knew there was definitely something happening that was broad scale and important but had not yet been named.

Paula: It was exciting. We fleshed out a work plan and began to talk with anyone who crossed our paths who was between forty-five and sixty-five.

Jeff: It wasn't a random sample, but we interviewed people across a wide range of socioeconomic levels, occupations, lifestyles, and geography.

Paula: We started with people we knew, and they introduced us to others. We posted a few requests on the Web, and as more people found out about the project, they found *us*. The stories were captivating.

Jeff: We talked with anyone who was willing about getting older and their plans for the future. We found that almost without exception, people were eager for the opportunity to tell us about the discomfort, sometimes panic, they were feeling about their next life stage. We have used many of their stories in this book, changing names and any identifying characteristics, but sharing the essential truths of what was told to us.

Paula: We were sometimes surprised but more often reassured as we heard others articulate and confirm the fears and doubts we were feeling, too. We began to see a clearly defined pattern. Children of the 1960s would reminisce for hours about the era in which they grew up. It was the *Big Chill* all over again. Except that now everyone was even older.

Jeff: It seemed as though people enjoyed talking about their past because it helped them understand their present. No matter how they had played their hands, it seemed to us that lives that began with so many options had inevitably come down to a well-trodden path and that what was once a very satisfying challenge was now merely obligation and inertia.

We also saw that inertia and depression were far from inevitable. We met boomers who creatively and courageously were facing these problems—head on. They refused to allow their choices to be limited by traditional expectations, and we were inspired by the breadth of choices some people were able to access. It became clear that "making choices" was the elixir of youth. Choice, we concluded, was the spark that fires energy—if you are courageous enough to reach for a new solution.

These tales of success are the motor of our narrative. They are the basis of some very practical guidance for a self-help program. No one person had all the answers, but it became clear that some specific areas of life need scrutiny if a new life plan is to be developed. Relationships with people, and with our bodies, as well as the role of work and the use of our money are all part of the new construction project.

Paula: Our own stories become part of the larger story. Both of us made some significant changes as a result of our explorations. Some of them were great—or we hope will be great. And most were very difficult.

Jeff: We will talk about the ups and downs of our own journeys and offer some suggestions for who and what to take with you on yours.

Paula: The people we spoke to had some good ideas about how to get your energy and body back and new ways to think about your money and work, which we found truly interesting—and think you will, too.

The Hourglass Solution is a manual for boomers who want to take back control of the rest of their lives. It will help them chart the way back to the excitement and enthusiasm of youth, guided by the experience of their years.

We have called this point of arrival Greater Adulthood. This part of adult life, we decided, needed a new name to differentiate it from where we are now.

There is a hard line between the years spent living out the choices made in one's twenties and thirties and the new course boomers can create for themselves between the ages of fifty and seventy. In Greater Adulthood, you reap the rewards of your hard work and life experience, but that reward is hardly a "long rest." It is a real life adventure story.

This book is your passport.

1

The Hourglass Effect: A Boomer Epidemic

Boomers are getting older, and they aren't taking it well. They aren't comfortable with the traditional roles that seniors have had in American life, and yet their "middle ages" have lost their glow as well. Too many boomers are stuck in lives that no longer excite them but see no other options.

At college reunions, weddings, funerals, and almost any other event where people of like age gather together, there is more than a hum of restlessness. There is thunderous discontent. Among people who appear to have achieved their goals and have reason for pride in accomplishment, there is often anxiety and palpable unhappiness. They are not looking forward to retirement, because they think it means loss of status—and loss of vitality. The early boomers who have tried it say it isn't even that much fun. But neither is the life they have been living. Boomers feel trapped in lives they created many years ago. The panic comes from a feeling of helplessness and the sense that life is no longer in their control. We call this the Hourglass Effect.

Adult life is made up of dozens of decisions in every arena. Some of them are big—like marriage or career or parenthood. Some decisions seem relatively small: buy a new car or save some money; take an exotic vacation or visit relatives. Some decisions are made daily: exercise or sleep late. For most people, the decisions that describe their life are a mixed bag of good calls and bad ones. Some course corrections are made along the way, but most adult lives have consistent themes.

The Hourglass Effect describes the cumulative impact of dozens of life choices and how these decisions can become a midlife straitjacket. It explains how even brilliant decisions that were very satisfying for decades can become a tightening noose of obligation and responsibility. Its most obvious symptom is a pervasive feeling of being *stuck* in a life that doesn't nourish basic needs. The consequences range from suicide to drug addiction to illness and depression. Although there are many different stories, there is a common theme, and it is about choice.

> **Paula:** The idea that the specific map of our life is defined by choices is a fundamental one. We tend to think about our lives in terms of consequences—as though those consequences were independent of the decisions we made along the way. The idea of life defined by choices made— and choices yet to be made—is highly liberating because it grants us control.
>
> **Jeff:** The way that we react to the issue of choice is very revealing. When we're young, choice means freedom. But once the breadth of options starts to diminish, some people lose the ability to see or even act on opportunities as they emerge

again. Making choices can become a true source
of anguish. "Choice anxiety" is real.

Each life stage has associated with it some cultural markers.
Some have been appropriated by religion such as christenings,
Bar Mitzvahs, and wedding celebrations. Other cultural markers are graduations, first jobs, promotions, anniversaries, the
birth of children, and home purchases. All these events signal
positive transformation, and they are about hope. They are
filled with expectations for the future and elicit a conditioned
and joyous response from others. Most significantly, these
markers are about positive choice.

This changes slowly; our fifties and sixties are marked by
losses: empty nest, downsizing, retirement, and deaths. None
of those markers are suggestive of choice, opportunity, love, adventure, or wealth. Quite the contrary, the vocabulary around
aging is about husbanding resources and pulling inward. Even
the inevitable illnesses are seen as much more negative in later
years. Young people work to recover. Older people learn to live
with it. Aging is a game of diminishing returns. This phase of
adulthood is also a time when boomers are likely to realize that
unless they reassess their personal situations and take additional
risks, their futures may not be all they had hoped for.

Boomers are unique in many ways, but most importantly,
they are addicted to the notion of a life of their own choosing.
Their particular generational history and their unique psychological imperatives (which we will discuss more fully in Chapter
2) make the idea that they have arrived at a place in life that has
few choices left nearly intolerable. Boomers who have achieved
enormous success, and those who have not, share a common
aversion to the notion that options run out in midlife. The idea

that life, even with the trophies they worked so hard to achieve, holds few choices for the future is terrifying.

> **Jeff:** Choice and control are inextricably linked. No matter how difficult the situation, people seem to be able to handle it with so much less anxiety if they feel they have made a choice, because that puts them in control.
>
> **Paula:** Yes, you can't always control the outcome, but nothing is worse than feeling like the victim of a situation that has overtaken you.
>
> **Jeff:** Boomers feel out of options and out of control.

The constraints on choice come from many directions. The job isn't as promising as it once was. Advancement is no longer the issue; hanging on is. Family life, while less hectic, leaves a lot more time for introspection. Top billing has been lost or stolen, almost overnight. It is the children's accomplishments that are the headlines, and most of the celebrations are theirs, with parents in the secondary role of Mother and Father of the Bride and Groom or silent benefactors. The events in which we are the central figure tend to mark endings rather than beginnings.

If there is movement at all, the trajectory of life takes a new and unfamiliar direction: retirement. There is a crushing finality even to the word itself. Is it a point of arrival or a totem of stagnation? *Retirement* literally means a period of withdrawal— to back away from activity. It comes with some heavy cultural baggage and has often meant an increased dependence on others. It may mean a loss of self-confidence, especially for the men and women of the baby-boom generation who have un-abashedly drawn much of their feelings of self-worth from their careers. For a generation that has always felt as though time was on its side, this juncture may evoke great anxiety and even fear about a future that is approaching much too fast.

> **Jeff:** It is, quite literally, "sickening." There is an epidemic affecting boomers that has both physical and psychological symptoms.
>
> **Paula:** We call it the Hourglass Effect because sufferers most frequently describe themselves as stuck—stuck in midlife.
>
> **Jeff:** We saw the problem as going from a big menu of options to a much reduced one. And we thought the solution must lie in making it wide again.

The physical symbol of the hourglass provides a new way of looking at life's timeline and another perspective on one's options. Instead of seeing the hourglass as a grim reminder of time slipping away, we can see it as representing the full life cycle of choice. The top of the hourglass suggests the breadth of possibility that boomers enjoyed as young adults. The narrow middle describes the restriction of options that was the inevitable result of making choices. The eventual widening of the bottom half of the hourglass provides a visual metaphor of choice and opportunity widening again. It holds the promise of a new life stage, which we call Greater Adulthood—the period in your life when the confluence of experience and self-knowledge is coupled with renewed energy for change. We'll talk more about Greater Adulthood in Chapter 2.

Our belief is that if one can get through the "stuck" phase, then the full breadth of choice will again be available, and with that will come the vitality that so many around us seemed to have lost. The fundamental premise of the Hourglass Solution is that a successful life is one in which we can make choices that allow us to stay in control of our own destiny. In other words, it is good to have options.

Now, right this minute, millions of boomers are approaching their fifties and sixties, and they are confronted with the very short list of well-established options for this part of life. James Firman, president of the National Council on Aging, spoke of this bluntly: "It's not like we have a lot of role models to show us the pathways. We're all lost as a generation. This is about reinventing yourself in a new stage of life. It's a gift— years of opportunity, years of health. But there's no clear path."[1]

Most say they feel uncertain about the next stage, and yet they find it hard to articulate alternatives. They feel anxious and confused, but they know they need to make plans. The media has been alerted: Each week, nearly every major magazine, newspaper, and TV station in the country has a bleak story about aging boomers.

Evidence that the Hourglass Effect is real is more than anecdotal. The social science literature is replete with new data documenting an alarmingly high level of stress and depression. Boomers appear to be suffering on virtually every measure of psychological trauma and sociological dislocation.

- A recent study at Columbia University discovered that depression is a major problem across all age groups but the highest incidence was among the middle-aged. This is the first study to definitely show that depression is a stronger risk factor, both physically and mentally, among the boomer population than among any other age group.[2]

- Midlife depression is not just an American problem. A 2007 study conducted jointly by Warwick University in Great Britain and Dartmouth College in the United States examined depression in eighty countries around the world. The results were amazingly consistent: Depression peaks at age forty-four—and doesn't reach the lower levels evidenced by young adults until age seventy.[3]

- Boomers are also prone to drug abuse and dependence. Illegal drug use is declining among teens, but it has been increasing among boomers—for several consecutive years. Illicit drug use among adults aged fifty to fifty-nine increased 63 percent from 2002 to 2005, and it is predicted that the number of drug-addicted Americans who are over fifty will soar from 1.7 million in 2008 to 4.4 million by 2020.[4]

- The most startling morbidity statistic of all is that 24 percent of boomers who died in 2003 (the last year the data was available) did not die of natural causes—by far the highest of any age group to die from nonnatural means.[5] Boomers are 26 percent of the population, but they accounted for nearly half of all drug-related deaths and over one-third of all suicides. In fact, boomers aged forty-five to fifty-four are nearly twice as likely to commit suicide as are teenagers.[6]

- More boomers die from motorcycle accidents than does
  any other age group. A surprising number die from extreme sports such as hang gliding and skydiving. Perhaps boomers are not yet admitting that their reaction
  times have slowed and their vision has faded.

As boomers get older, some are experiencing a breakdown
of the social bonds that gave their life meaning. The job that
used to be so important has disappeared—or, at the very least,
is less exciting. Marriages fall apart or go stale. The work of
child rearing is over. For many of us, this trifecta—work, a primary relationship, and children—have been the major forces
that have guided our behavior. Detachment from the normaliz-
ing patterns of everyday life is a major cause of depression, and
in extreme cases, the detachment from these life contracts can
result in suicide.

Don Blazer, Duke University professor of psychiatry and
behavioral science specializing in geriatrics, does not predict a
comfortable transition for boomers in the coming years: "Since
adolescence, they've been drinking and using more drugs than
previous generations. They're less likely to have strong religious
beliefs, more isolated, [experiencing] twice the divorce rate of
the generation before them and still facing money and work issues they thought would be behind them in their sixties. This is
not going to be an easy period for boomers as they age."[7]

> **Paula:** We do have to acknowledge that not all
> boomers are on the brink of suicide. Many actu-
> ally enjoy their grandchildren, enjoy making plans
> about their future.

Jeff: Absolutely. But generally, those are the people who see midlife as an opportunity for renewal and growth. Denial and resistance to change are bound to create unhappy surprises.

Paula: Right. Everything has a shelf life. Significant change at work and at home is inevitable. Some people weather these changes cheerfully, but for most, the emotional cost is considerable.

In the landmark research project "Midlife in the U.S. (MIDUS)," funded by the MacArthur Foundation, one college-educated respondent put it succinctly. In answer to the question "What are your hopes for the future?" she responded, "To be able to make choices. To have circumstances and the ability to make choices in your life. Not to be in a position where you have to do something because you have no choice."[8]

Inevitably, those who have made choices and see that they are not trapped are the ones who are happiest, no matter what choices they actually made. It is the absence of choice that defines depression.

Choice is the essence of the Hourglass Solution. Access to choice defines the broad part of the hourglass and the feeling of optimism and well-being that affords control over one's life. The absence of choice is what we call the neck of the hourglass: the sense of being trapped—stuck in a life stage over which one has lost control. It is the condition that makes aging anathema in our culture. Choice is especially important in the United States, where independence is highly valued and critical to personal health. And it is vital to baby boomers, who cut their teeth on the notion that a cornucopia of choice is their entitlement.

Mental and even physical health is highly correlated with the perception of being in command of one's life and able to influence outcome. Although the benefits of autonomy are evident across the adult life span, the relationship between control and well-being is especially strong in later adulthood, where losses can become more numerous and wins less frequent.

There is a strong correlation between advancing age and the need for control. Young children expect that parents will be in control, and this expectation contributes to the child's sense of safety. But they also anticipate that they will be rewarded with greater control as they get older. This is the apocryphal dialectic between parent and child: Parents draw the line, and children must try to cross it. Children assert their desire for control at various junctures, and their sense of well-being is affected by their ability to gain control as appropriate. In healthy adults, the need for control over one's own life decisions increases, and the ability to exercise that control is a major factor in adult happiness. In the forties, fifties, and sixties, this need for personal control is especially strong.

> **Jeff:** Control is associated with better health and well-being and is the essential element determining the quality of later life.[9] I could fill the room with corroborative evidence.
>
> **Paula:** Even anecdotally, older adults who have autonomy and control are seen as aspirational. What is scary is watching people give up on themselves. It may start with the quality of their surroundings—and ends with the loss of passion for life.

A successful and complete life necessarily includes the presumption of usefulness and competence and a level of control over one's environment, but the most important factor may be the continued ability to make choices. The phenomenon we have described as the Hourglass Effect is the opposite: It marks the loss of control that accompanies the inability to identify choices. This is the malaise now affecting boomers in large numbers. In psychological terms, it is despair and stagnation. In daily conversations, people call it "stuck."

Too many boomers believe that the choices they made in the first forty or fifty years of their lives have predetermined the trajectory of the second. They are paralyzed by the lack of control they feel over what appears to be their destiny. They don't want what they have—and they don't yet know what it will take to make them feel, once again, fulfilled and optimistic and in the driver's seat. They fear change and they fear the future, because they don't have a new template for the rest of their lives.

2

Boomerology:
The Generational Experience

Relinquishing power and surrendering the prerogatives of youth are not in the boomer lexicon. Every aspect of their collective experience since childhood militates against a graceful and gradual retreat. Boomers are not prepared socially or emotionally for the model of aging and retirement that exists in our culture today and that is largely about surrender and loss.

Boomers must invent a new model. Their unique history, their large numbers, and their collective consciousness create the imperative for a different view of this life stage, and the context for new forms. Seventy-five million people are entering midlife with the accumulated wisdom of five decades of invention and experimentation and the bonus of largely undiminished physical energy.

This chapter will discuss the signature events of the boomer experience and the social environment that created an unprecedented array of options available to baby boomers in nearly every aspect of their lives. The availability of choices, a generational bias toward self-actualization, and an addiction to center-stage demands the reengineering of traditional views of midlife and aging.

As boomers entered young adulthood, the top of the hourglass of opportunity was broader than it had ever been in human history. Men and women of all races enjoyed access to innumerable educational institutions, career opportunities, and financial rewards. In politics, music, and fashion, the agenda of boomers became the agenda for the nation. The culture of the country was focused on youth in unprecedented ways. And boomers developed a lifelong appetite for being the center of attention.

The Vietnam War was one of many battlegrounds for boomers and may have been the most enduring one. Although only 9.7 percent of eligible boomer men served in Vietnam and surprisingly few boomers actually were activists, it was the defining issue for the generation.[1]

The Vietnam War was polarizing on the basis of class and age. The oldest and the poorest of the generation went to war. When troop buildup increased in the mid-1960s, the oldest boomers were just reaching the draftable age of eighteen. Of the men sent to Vietnam, 76 percent were from lower-middle-class and working-class backgrounds.[2] College deferments for the middle class became ubiquitous in the mid-1960s, but the threat of the draft personalized the war even for those who would never serve.

The spring of 1968 saw an unprecedented chain of events. President Lyndon Baines Johnson declined to run for a second term, largely because the divisiveness of the war threatened to topple not just his administration but also the Democratic Party. Within months, both Martin Luther King and Bobby

Kennedy were assassinated. Young people across the political spectrum saw their hopes for the future shatter. This culminated in the riots at the Democratic Convention in Chicago in1968, which effectively destroyed the left wing of the Democratic Party and assured victory for the Republicans. The killings at Kent State in 1970 and, ultimately, the fall of Saigon put a punctuation point on a political environment dominated by the participation of young people and their agenda—a level of participation that has not been seen since then. Despite the influence of younger generations on the candidacy of Barack Obama in 2008, we have yet to witness an activism of the ferocity of the Vietnam era.

Paula: It is hard to overestimate the indelible imprint of those days. The immediacy of world events to young people has not been experienced on such a broad scale since. The Iraq War is only real to the men and women in the military—and their families. For those of us who came of age in the 1960s, politics was in the drinking water. My boyfriend burned his draft card and went to Canada. I was in the antiwar movement, and so was everyone I knew. It was a life-changing experience to be part of a movement that had such a direct impact on world events.

Jeff: I was in high school when the draft became a critical issue. I registered like everybody else I knew and got number 116 in the draft lottery—not a good number.[3] In my head, 116 will always be one of my personal numbers—like my birthday or social security number. As I got closer

to graduation, I applied for conscientious objec-
tor status.

Paula: It was a time when all the lines were hard
lines. There were no abstentions. Everyone chose a
side. Whatever side you were on—for the war or
against it—other choices were made by default.

Although a very small number of boomers were actually involved in antiwar activities (roughly around 10 percent) and an
even smaller number participated in the Chicago riots or
joined the Weathermen, yippies, or Students for a Democratic
Society (SDS), the cumulative impact of the Vietnam War on
the psychosocial dynamics of the generation cannot be over-
stated. The experience of the 1960s gave boomers a common
context—no matter what their actual political beliefs were.
Their distinctive music and style of dress identified the army of
boomers to one another—as well as to the rest of the world—
for decades to come.

One profound effect of the war in Vietnam for boomers
was skepticism about government. Whether they landed as
Democrats or Republicans, boomers did not emerge from this
experience with an abiding faith in our institutions. If they
served in the war, many were embittered by their country's lack
of support for their sacrifice. If they did not serve, they maintained a lifelong skepticism about the motivations of our political leaders. The members of the Vietnam generation learned
the power of protest and saw the impact of their numbers on
national events. But most importantly, they would live the rest
of their lives with institutions that had been irrevocably damaged by the experience.

Tarnished institutions do not have the same impact on social behavior as revered ones do. Laws were broken in very public ways during the protests of the 1960s: Draft cards were burned, and private property was damaged. Whether it was experienced live or viewed on television, all Americans witnessed a broad-scale change in conventional behavior that ranged from men with long hair, to very public displays of affection, to recreational drugs. A rock festival held in Woodstock, New York, in 1969 became iconic for the counterculture. Most estimates of attendance hover around five hundred thousand. For some, it was a festival of peace and love and harmony. For others, it was a glimpse into a Dante's *Inferno* of hedonism. But like the political demonstrations of the period, it was emblematic of a generation that was defying social convention at every turn. A Pandora's box of social behavior was opened, and with that came options. The top of the hourglass was broader than it had ever been. Choices became an entitlement for an entire generation. Control over one's own life was an inalienable right.

> **Paula:** The habit of choosing became endemic. There were very few parental or even societal injunctions that were accepted without question. I can conjure up a very bratty picture of myself at nineteen or twenty. My response to nearly any request—particularly from an adult— was "It's my choice."
>
> **Jeff:** I can imagine you being bratty. But for me, and my brothers as well, parental authority was to be resisted on all fronts. My poor mother— there were seven of us.

The cultural environment of the late 1960s gave boomers a blank permission slip—permission to defy the government and institutional authority and permission to redefine the entire range of social behavior, from gender roles to sexual orientation. Sex was no longer the prerogative of only married people, and indeed, the entire institution of marriage was reexamined. Instead of marriage being a universal passage, it, too, became a choice and a battleground for control.

The World War II generation had significant prohibitions embedded in its collective consciousness about sex without marriage. The advent of the birth control pill in 1960 and its broad availability to young people changed this forever. It was not just that the Pill could be relied on to prevent pregnancy, but also that it separated decisions about sex from decisions about reproduction. Birth control became a decision made by women and controlled by women and, once and for all, gave them control over nature. In the 1970s, ten million American women were using the Pill. This created options that no other generation of females had ever experienced. Most significantly, women now had the option to delay marriage and to plan childbearing.

> **Paula:** Those two things—permission not to marry and permission to have sex without fear of pregnancy—changed everything for my generation. The women's movement developed momentum in the early 1970s, and I don't think it would have happened without the Pill.
>
> **Jeff:** And the antiwar movement wouldn't have happened without the draft. Both were political expressions of a generational insistence on having

control that the previous generation was willing
to entrust to government . . . or biology . . .
    Paula: Or luck.

The 1973 *Roe v. Wade* Supreme Court decision to allow abortion unleashed a debate that continues to this day. The debate concerns a woman's right to choose and her right to control reproduction. This issue equals the Vietnam War in its power to polarize public opinion and influence the political agenda of the nation. The vocabulary of choice and control became part of the generational dialogue in a more overt way than ever before. The members of this generation, more than those who came before them, saw themselves not just as actors, but also as the directors of the broader cultural scene. The feeling that they could effect significant social change was perhaps the most enduring legacy of the 1960s.

Although most boomers obeyed the reigning social mores and ultimately settled into traditional marriages and had children in the conventional manner, the idea that choice and control could be exercised in one's personal life released a genie from the lamp. It redefined an entire generation.

Boomers did face obstacles associated with many of their nontraditional choices. Women in the workplace faced discriminatory practices and role confusion. Two-career families faced stresses unknown to their parents. Delayed childbearing meant fertility problems for millions. Boomers came to understand that every choice comes with its own set of issues. Nonetheless, at a very formative life stage, they learned that it wasn't necessary to do things as their parents and grandparents had done them. Almost any social or psychological convention was subject to challenge. If one decided to depart from historic norms, there was bound to be a crowd of fellow boomers with whom you could find community.

Demography has played a significant role in boomer destiny at every life stage. Seventy-five million strong, boomers are the largest generation in America and will continue to be so for the next fifteen to twenty years. Size is its own kind of power. Populations typically resemble a pyramid, with the most populous group, babies, at the bottom and the elderly at the top. This has not been the case with boomers, who continue to outnumber all subsequent generations. For the first time in U.S. history, there are more fifty-year-olds than thirty-five-year-olds, and more people over sixty than those under five.

This generation has been called "the pig in the python" by demographers. From the time boomers were born, the force of their numbers strained and reshaped many of our country's institutions, from public schools to welfare rolls. The pig-in-the-python has continued to move and is now poised to place unprecedented pressure on the social security and Medicare systems. The experience of the 1960s provides boomers with a bias toward activism and an unstated, though widespread, belief that their agenda should be a high priority for the nation.

Young people have always had more choices and more decisions to make than the very old. But in previous generations, powerful social forces were understood to be a mitigating factor that helped to define alternatives. The impact of social class, race, and gender were expected to serve as guidelines for the choices made by the young—simply by limiting the options.

Significant changes in social institutions at a macro level in America after World War II dramatically altered the nature of choices available to young people. These changes expanded the breadth of opportunity available to the men and women of

World War II, and these options multiplied geometrically for their children, the boomer generation. The cumulative impact was nothing less than explosive.

For the World War II generation, the impact of the draft and the GI Bill, which made higher education available to hundreds of thousands of young men who might ordinarily have never gone to college, had a flattening effect on American society. Where higher education had formerly been the entitlement of only the wealthy, it now was available to all the young men returning from the war—regardless of social class. This fundamentally changed the class structure for the World War II generation, but even more profoundly for their children—the boomers.

Eighty-nine percent of boomers completed high school—almost triple the percentage of their parents. And 28 percent of boomers had a bachelor's degree or higher, nearly quadruple the rate of the previous generation. The number of college students tripled between 1965 and 1975.[4]

The GI Bill and the accessibility of education, irrevocably changed the educational establishment and blurred class distinctions that had channeled and directed the choices of young people for hundreds of years. As they came to maturity, boomers had many more options than their parents had in choosing their occupation and their mate.

Compounding the impact of education on the class structure, the postwar period also saw dramatic changes in the political realities of race and, subsequently, gender in American life. In 1954, the U.S. Supreme Court ruled on *Brown v. Board of Education*. This was the first of many steps aimed at removing the racially based obstacles to the entitlements of U.S. citizenship. The case itself was about the widespread practice of segregating black children in separate schools throughout the country. The ruling declared that the policy of enforced separate education could not be construed as granting equal access and was therefore unconstitutional. The decision's significance went far beyond school desegregation, although it occasioned the forcible integration of public schools in the South.

In 1957, President Dwight Eisenhower deployed the 101st Airborne to Little Rock, Arkansas, after Governor Orval Faubus ordered the National Guard to block the entry of black children to formerly all-white Central High School. In 1963, Governor George Wallace personally stood in the doorway of the University of Alabama attempting to bar black students from entering. Many early baby boomers watched these events unfold on television in what was to become the first of many shared historic events, made possible through the ubiquity of television news.

Although *Brown v. Board of Education* did not end racial discrimination in America, its significance for boomers is that for this generation, racial equality became a standard enforced by law. For boomers, at the very least, people of all races were visible in most aspects of their daily life. The process of integration had begun. Blacks and whites went to school together, rode public transportation together, and served in the armed forces together. This was not true for previous generations.

The Civil Rights Act of 1964 was another critical step in the process and guaranteed that neither race nor gender could be used to deprive any American from exercising options pertaining to education, employment, and housing. As active participants in the struggle for civil rights, as beneficiaries, or merely as witnesses, the baby boom generation had experiences different from those of their parents and grandparents. These historic milestones were of more-than-passing significance. Equality before the law was part of the air this generation breathed. This set the stage for a host of other entitlements.

> **Paula:** Our behavior in the workplace surely was affected. I suspect boomers were much quicker to identify bias and much more vocal about it than previous generations. We were empowered to expect "fair" treatment, and demand it when it was not forthcoming.
>
> **Jeff:** The ascendance of Hillary Clinton and Sarah Palin and the election of Barack Obama were events that sealed the deal for millions of Boomers.

Health, Wealth, and Happiness

The children of the postwar baby boom had every reason to take good health for granted. Childhood inoculations against smallpox were ubiquitous, as was protection from diphtheria, measles, rubella, and a host of other diseases that had so often been fatal in the not-too-distant past.

Finally, in 1955, the Salk vaccine for polio became broadly available, thus eliminating one of the most feared childhood illnesses of previous decades. It is hard to overestimate the significance of this vaccine. More than the number of children it protected, the availability of the vaccine heralded a new era of preventive medicine, which perhaps laid the foundation for the boomer generation's trust in the medical community.

Coincident was the "outsourcing" of health care to professionals on a much broader scale than ever before. Whereas care for the sick had traditionally been a family responsibility, the availability and dependence on health-care professionals became part of the fabric of American life. Well-baby visits to pediatricians and annual checkups, dental appointments, and eye exams contributed to the notion that good health was not a matter of faith or luck; it was the result of smart choices made possible by good science and access to professional care. Boomers expected to have both. The presumption of health forged a kind of courage, sometimes recklessness, that opened doors to travel, sexual experimentation, and faith in drugs (both prescription and otherwise).

> **Paula:** Attitudes about health have been transformed so dramatically in my lifetime. Before the polio vaccine, we weren't allowed to go to public pools in the summer. If we were sick, we just stayed home. By the time my kids were born, they were vaccinated against everything.
>
> **Jeff:** Growing up in a large family, I saw enormous changes from my oldest to my youngest brothers. In the 1940s, my mother had two still-born children, and then my oldest brother died of childhood leukemia at the age of six. My next oldest brothers had the same experiences as you did, Paula, but by the time I was in school, polio had all but disappeared and there was fluoride in the drinking water. We believed that medical science could overcome just about anything. Of course, we were wrong.

AIDS, one of the greatest health crises ever, was an anomalous event for the preventive-medicine generation. An incurable disease that affected those in the prime of life on such a broad scale was outside our previous frame of reference. Perhaps for that reason, the lethal impact of the HIV virus was hard to accept at first, even for those who were the most at risk. The history of the epidemic is in many ways emblematic of the social changes that have defined the boomer generation: It required all Americans to acknowledge the gay community and helped some people to embrace a collective cause. HIV/AIDS continues to be at the front line of political and medical activism powered by the generational belief in science. The demand for a cure and the expectation that it will be delivered continues undaunted by the obstacles.

The mobilization of the gay community and its ability to exercise political, and even scientific, pressure was a marker event in the history of sexual orientation as much as the epidemiology of the disease itself. Again, boomers had made an impact on the national agenda.

The sense of control over one's body and physical health was irrevocably shaken, but not surrendered to the AIDS epidemic. Since childhood, this generation has understood that illness was curable, that biological functions were manipulatable, and that physical characteristics could be altered for fashion or convenience. Even AIDS has not blunted that belief.

Members of this generation had their noses "fixed" as teenagers and their breasts augmented in their twenties and thirties. Men as well as women cosmetically enhanced their appearance—grew hair, capped teeth, and pulled and puffed out wrinkles. Even more fundamental, this generation defied its biology through chemistry—first with the Pill and later with fertility drugs that facilitated delayed childbearing to nearly biblical extremes.

Boomers have a different relationship with their bodies than did previous generations, who thought that nature should not be trifled with. Cures for menopause, erectile dysfunction, baldness, failing eyesight, and general sagginess are ubiquitous. Since the mid-1990s, there has been a 446 percent increase in cosmetic surgery, which was a $12 billion industry in 2007.[5]

Boomers have also developed an almost sci-fi comfort with part replacement: liver, kidney, heart, knee, and hips. The incidence of such surgeries has been increasing at the rate of 10 percent or more per year, and it is estimated that as many as twenty million Americans carry artificial organs or transplants.[6] Some scientists predict that eventually all organs will become replaceable one day.

It is reasonable to assume that as more boomers experience the debilitating effects of aging, more products, drugs, and surgeries will become available to negate these problems. What is unlikely is that people will passively accept infirmity as inevitable.

Although the United States has never approached a state of economic equality, the boom of the 1960s granted the children of the World War II generation a degree of financial security and access to lifestyle choices that historically was the province of a very few. By any measure, boomers are the richest generation in history, whether you look at the trillion dollars they spend every year on goods and services or the annual average household income of over seventy thousand dollars.[7]

Beyond mere dollar amounts, the American Dream became available to a vastly wider swath of the population than ever before. The poverty rate for boomers is now 7.3 percent and by far the lowest of any segment of the population, whereas home ownership is 78 percent, the highest of any age group.[8] For most of the baby boom generation, food, clothing, a family car, and bikes for the kids came with the territory.

Traditionally, spending patterns of senior citizens became more conservative. As they "retired" from society, they earned less and spent less. Their discretionary funds were often used to help children and grandchildren. Baby boomers have turned this pattern upside down. Instead of spending less as they get older, boomers are spending more. In fact, as boomers age, they tend to spend more and more on themselves with each passing year. The average member of a fifty-plus household spends nineteen thousand dollars per year; this is 30 percent more than the average member of an under-fifty household.[9] Even if the recession of 2008 persists, we are likely to see the age disparity continue.

An additional point of difference is how we save. For members of the previous generation, for whom the Depression was still vivid, saving was an important element in their feelings of optimism and security for the future. Saving made them feel good. Deferred gratification was a point of pride.

> **Jeff:** This is a very significant point. Whether this is a function of the expectation of longevity or a lifetime addiction to shopping, it's hard to say, but boomers spend like there's no tomorrow.
>
> **Paula:** Is it denial? A lack of awareness that there will come a time when their earning power is diminished—or even nonexistent?
>
> **Jeff:** I think it is all those things. Also, most boomers have known only relative prosperity and

increasing income. It is hard to imagine what you
have never experienced.

Paula: We will see if the current economic climate has an impact on boomer spending habits,
but if the past is a predictor of the future, it seems
unlikely.

Jeff: In fact, just the opposite seems to be true.
Even though boomers are more concerned than
ever about money for retirement, they are not doing much about it. Maybe you're right: It is denial.

For boomers, consumer spending is an entitlement and a
form of self-expression. While their parents practiced spending
restraint and the virtues of frugality, boomers learned from an
early age that products of all kinds could provide emotional
satisfaction and had the capacity to give meaning to their lives.
They learned that certain brands telegraphed vital information
about themselves and that retail therapy was at least a temporary conduit to happiness and even to feelings of self-worth.

Reared on television and suburban shopping malls,
boomers are sponges for modern marketing. They wear the
logos of prestigious brands and are insulted when the pitches
seem to slow down. The American Association for Retired Per-
sons (AARP), the largest boomer organization in the country,
has blasted advertisers for ignoring boomers and not catering
to their consumer needs. AARP has been running an ad cam-
paign of its own, demanding that marketers aim more advertising toward the lucrative boomer target and asking corporations
to design more products specifically for boomers to buy.

Boomers have been the driving engine of the American
economy for several decades, and they aren't done yet. Some 70

percent of the nation's net worth is in their hands, and they control half of all household discretionary spending.[10] They spend twice as much on consumer goods and services as do young adults. In other words, in addition to political power and control of social institutions, boomers still have their hands on the throttle of economic power. The choices boomers make about their money will define a personal Hourglass Solution, but collectively their decisions will drive the American economy.

The spending habits of boomers is only one element of their quest for happiness—a condition that boomers have relentlessly pursued throughout their entire lives. Therapy, meditation, exercise, and drugs—anything that makes them feel good—is an option. Previous generations viewed happiness as a fleeting state of grace; boomers aspire to it as a life state. For boomers, happiness is emotional real estate. Once achieved, it is owned until it is sold or squandered. If lost, the pursuit begins again. Members of this generation are not content with nostalgia. Nor do they believe that in their old age, they can be sustained by their memories.

Martin Seligman, noted psychologist, author, and professor at the University of Pennsylvania, has been studying the notion of human happiness for over thirty years. "Boomers' obsession with self-esteem leads them to believe that there is something fundamentally wrong with those who don't feel good about themselves—all the time. Individuals can quite easily will themselves into a state of depression by believing that they should feel better than they do—whereas they may simply be feeling 'normal.'"[11]

The preoccupation with happiness is not a pursuit that they have come to in middle age—it has been lifelong—and this is not coincidence. Notions of childhood change throughout history as a function of politics, life expectancy, and technology. The idea of a "happy childhood" began in the 1950s.

Prior to the war, the childhood years may have been thought of as relatively carefree, but the accompanying emotional state was hardly foremost in the minds of parents or educators. Childhood was brief and, depending on social class, either an economic adjunct or a prep course for what lay ahead.

Not so in the 1950s. Central to the idyllic notions about the nuclear family was the concept of "happy" children. In fact, happiness was a critical function of children at this time. No longer a necessary part of the labor force, they played a central role in the developing family style of the postwar generation. "Happy children" testified to the success of child-centered parenting. Happiness was the domestic product of the 1950s and 1960s.

> **Paula:** I grew up in a very child-centered family. My mom was a crusader in Dr. Spock's happy, whole-child movement. Unhappy children were an implicit indictment—of the kid but also the mother.
>
> **Jeff:** It was an age of happiness. Everything in the culture insisted that the 1950s and even the early 1960s was just the greatest time to be a kid. The Beaver and Wally never had a problem Mom and Dad couldn't handle. The Mouseketeers lived in Disneyland—it didn't get better than that.
>
> **Paula:** And yet, of course, that wasn't true. Our childhoods were no safer or happier, but there was enormous pressure to present it that way.
>
> **Jeff:** Sickness, war, and threats to national security or the environment were the concerns of the

fringe like Rachel Carson and Ralph Nader. My brothers and I did dig a makeshift bomb shelter in our backyard—mostly because we thought it was cool and we could hide from our parents. We really didn't believe that anyone was going to attack Seattle.

Boomers learned that happiness is another entitlement and have been unwilling to accept unhappiness as anything but a temporary obstacle. Boomers meditate, medicate, go to therapy, and join support groups. Perhaps in the end, they are no more content than other cohort groups—but the idea that happiness is an attainable and sustainable emotional state has colored every aspect of their existence to date. They expect to be happy at home, at work, and with themselves. They desperately want to be happy with their own aging, as well. The idea that their best years are behind them is abhorrent.

Florida State University history professor Darrin M. McMahon explains this new take on happiness: "It's only relatively recently that human beings have begun to think of happiness as not just an earthly possibility, but also in some ways as an obligation or entitlement, a natural human right. This has had an unintended effect. When we think of happiness as our natural condition—the way we ought to be—then it becomes natural to blame ourselves or others when we are not happy, as if somehow we've been done an injustice or done something wrong ourselves. I think this has created a new and very modern pressure, even a new type of unhappiness: I call it the unhappiness of not being happy."[12]

The search for self-fulfillment and meaning has reached new heights among this generation. Although psychologist

Abraham Maslow developed his theory of self-actualization in the 1940s and found his first audience among the postwar intelligentsia, the broad-scale preoccupation with self-actualization occurred in the 1960s.[13] In fact, self-actualization, with the attendant focus on personal growth and fulfillment, became a mantra for those who came of age in the 1960s and 1970s. Self-help groups, from consciousness-raising for women to est (Erhard Seminars Training) and the transcendental-meditation movement, proliferated to fuel what became a generational obsession with one's own psychological state.

Maslow was quite explicit that only 2 percent of the adult population could ever achieve self-actualization. But in the popularized version that boomers hungrily consumed, it became an entitlement. Now, thirty-five years since the emergence of the cult of self-fulfillment, the vocabulary has evolved but the obsession continues. We seriously doubt that this generation will slide gracefully into a new life stage that doesn't hold out a promise of a better, richer sense of self.

What's Next

There is one overriding reason why boomers simply can't accept the traditional paradigm of aging—they expect more from life than any previous generation. The result of historic changes in American life is that baby boomers entered adulthood with unprecedented access and options. They developed a bias toward having multiple choices for just about everything. The educational system, the social environment, and relative prosperity created a predilection for the availability of options in all areas of life.

Building on these generational attitudes, boomers have defined the approach to every life stage they have moved through. They expect to be in control. They want to make a difference. They insist on happiness and self-actualization, and they presume that they will manage even the physical changes that accompany aging. Their experience of heightened expectations has changed the way they approach relationships and family, their outlook on work, and their behavior toward their own bodies. It is just these habits of a lifetime that will provide boomers with the tools to renovate the next life stage.

Boomers want to continue to influence the political landscape and have meaningful roles in the workplace and the marketplace. They may want to again rearrange family patterns and traditional living arrangements. And they want to take back some territory in the physical battle against aging. The questions we will explore in the chapters that follow is, "Is this reasonable?" and "Is this possible?"

Greater Adulthood

Jeff: Our audacious answer is *yes*. We believe that by summoning the skills and disciplines honed through a lifetime of effort, boomers will find some answers that will suit them at least as well as the lives they have made so far. Some have done so already.

Paula: The key to the fifties and sixties is not to "extend" middle age—it is about finding the path to Greater Adulthood. Greater Adulthood is a new life stage that is so different in contour, it requires a new name. It is the years between fifty and seventy, in which boomers, pioneering a new course for themselves, can expect great opportunities and new satisfaction. In Greater Adulthood, one is not without options.

Jeff: Every life stage that boomers have successfully negotiated has required time, patience, and the support of others. This was true in childhood, in adolescence, and throughout young adulthood. That same attention is required now. Boomers can invent a new life stage—they've done it before. In their twenties, they were the first generation to leave home and live on their own—postparents and premarriage. This was unprecedented. Forging a new life stage is in the boomer lexicon.

Paula: Greater Adulthood is truly the promise of something better. It just takes some work to get there. It took energy and commitment to go to college, get married, buy a house, and have kids. Greater Adulthood will be no less challenging.

Boomers must revisit the defining decisions in their lives and reevaluate their options. Some will again choose the path they have pursued for thirty years. Others will select radically different solutions—but the very act of choosing will provide ballast for weathering those situations that are not in their hands. Events may not always be in their control, but creative and relevant solutions not only are available, but also are the legacy of all that boomers have experienced and accomplished to date.

It is the feeling that they are stuck in an old footprint, without the choices and sense of control they have come to expect, that has created their current crisis.

3

Stuck in the Hourglass:
The Straitjacket of Midlife

The idea that a successful life is filled with challenge and excitement and that every year could be better than the last is in boomers' generational DNA. Nevertheless, many boomers have reached a tipping point at which obligation and responsibility have replaced choice and control. Sometimes it's relationships that are no longer nourishing; sometimes it is a job that is no longer rewarding. In Chapter 1, we described the depression and other physical manifestations of the Hourglass Effect, but often it is a far less specific feeling, like an illness that stretches ahead in a long, bleak line. This is the crisis we have called "stuck in the neck of the hourglass."

Getting stuck happens so slowly, and over time, it can feel like a natural and inevitable state. Expectations erode, and the strong sense of self that is the power of youth stagnates. It is the cause of inner conflict, depression, and anxiety. This is a difficult platform from which to launch a bold, new adventure. The people you will meet in this chapter live in the neck of the hourglass. Some have succumbed to despair, others double up on antidepressants, but all are disabled by the Hourglass Effect.

The symptoms are everywhere, but sometimes it is difficult to put a name on the diagnosis. Often it is expressed as a desperate need to appear younger than we are. Sometimes it pushes us to take foolish risks. Often we lash out at those closest to us as we seek to assign blame. But most often, it is just a generalized loss of vitality and a subconscious undercurrent of wistful dissatisfaction. Because the Hourglass Effect can incubate for years before it turns critical, we have found that ordinary conversations can be particularly revealing and helpful in identifying the problem.

From a psychological point of view, language and cognition are intertwined. Complex thoughts and feelings are constructed and synthesized through the use of language. In other words, one's experiences are a function of the language one uses to describe them. Sociolinguists like Deborah Tannen have demonstrated that language is a series of cultural data points.[1] The repeated use of words and phrases that imply helplessness in multiple situations by a generation that has always seen itself as powerful is what helped us identify the phenomena of the Hourglass Effect. The words we use disclose more than just their objective meaning. The *language of stuck* is ubiquitous:

"I'm too old to change."

"I'm too old to learn something new."

"There's nothing I can do about it."

"I don't *want* to. I *have* to."

"I don't have a choice."

Paula: Every one of those phrases, we heard more than once. Phrases like "I have no choice" communicate powerlessness. Feeling helpless is a symptom of being stuck.

Jeff: If you keep saying that you have "no choice," it will inhibit your ability to see options. If you keep saying "I have to" instead of "I want to," you will begin to see yourself as a victim.

Paula: When people talked about their relationships, their bodies, and their work, the language of stuck was an indication to us that there was a problem—as you will see as our story unfolds.

Jeff: Many people we spoke with were, by all external standards, living the life they had always dreamed about. We were often surprised by their stories. The strongest achievers were sometimes the most profoundly stuck because their success was accompanied by numerous obligations.

Quick had been an attorney in Charlotte for twenty-four years and was one of North Carolina's top one hundred lawyers for the past five. He was tall, trim, and handsome-looking, perhaps more like a TV news anchor or game-show host than a hard-nosed corporate litigator. One couldn't imagine him in anything other than a perfectly tailored suit—probably Ralph Lauren—unless he was on the golf course, and then definitely in Ralph Lauren. He had a successful career with money to spare and two beautiful daughters—both in college and both engaged. If you knew Quick, he might well be the last person you would predict would feel trapped in midlife at the age of forty-eight.

"Being a lawyer came naturally to me," he said, "which was fortunate because my father, grandfather, and any male in my family you could trace back to the Civil War was a lawyer. Heritage and tradition are important in the South, almost as important as what church you go to and who you marry." When Quick got divorced, about two years before we first spoke with him, he knew that it was going to be a difficult transition, but he found out that it affected his well-constructed life more than he could possibly have imagined. It had nothing to do with companionship. Quick had more blind dates—and quite a few great ones, he told us—than he could fit on his calendar. The issue for Quick was that he had to confront his future in a way that he had never considered before.

"I have absolutely no idea what I am going to do for the rest of my life. When I was married, it was easy to fool myself into thinking that I was happy. Maybe I didn't love my work, but I knew who I was doing it for—my wife and daughters. Now I realize that I should be doing it for myself, and it scares the heck out of me—because I really can't stand the thought of being a lawyer for another seventeen years. What they show you on *Boston Legal* and *LA Law* is a lie. Being a lawyer is boring, political, and competitive. The work is basically reading thousands of pages of legal crap and saying no—that's what a lawyer does. It's repetitive and dull."

Quick's lifestyle and his role in Charlotte society have conspired to paint him into a corner. Alimony, rent, college tuition, country club dues, and clothing bills make a sudden move to another career a greater risk than Quick is psychologically prepared to take. "I'm really frightened," he admitted.

"I'm not seeing a psychiatrist yet, and I'm not taking anything stronger than aspirin, and I don't drink more than a few martinis. But there are days I just can't hold it together. And I really need to figure that out before I do something stupid."

Jeff: When we pressed Quick to imagine what his life might be like at sixty-five or seventy, he responded uncharacteristically tersely, "I have no goddamn idea. And I don't want to think about it."

Paula: "I don't want to think about it" is right out of the language of the stuck phrase book. It is often very difficult for people to admit that they have reached a point in their lives where they are at an impasse. For some, an admission of unhappiness, reduced expectations, depression, or discontent is an embarrassing exposure of personal weakness.

Jeff: One by-product of the achievement-oriented, success-driven scorecard for young adulthood is the winner-loser mentality. Winners are strivers and damn happy about it. Losers wallow and whine. This makes it hard to come out and talk about your problems.

Paula: Until now, stuck in the neck of the hourglass was a "problem that had no name," like feminist Betty Friedan's description of the malaise of the housewife in the 1950s. In both cases, sufferers often self-medicated with drugs, alcohol, or frantic activity or gradually withdrew. Or like James, they took more drastic action.

James grew up in the suburbs of Chicago and graduated from Northwestern University in 1970, just in time to enlist in the U.S. Marine Corps and go to Vietnam. After five years in the service, his engineering degree in hand, he returned to the States and joined a major defense contractor in Washington, D.C. He married the first girl he dated in college, had one son, and was, by all accounts, very, very happy. The stars seemed to further align when he was promoted to run his company's regional office in St. Louis.

His life made sense. Most of his friends were either former marines or work buddies, and he was close with quite a few. But such relationships can fade over time, given the demands of family life. His wife, Sarah, a homemaker, expected him home every night at seven, and she needed him on weekends. She provided the vocabulary for an idealized family life and insisted that they stick close to the script. "We are so happy" she frequently said to James and everyone else. Her view was bulletproof—it was not offered up for discussion.

The furrow he had dug for himself was far narrower than he realized. It was a trench. He had no friends outside work and no passionate interests or hobbies. He had no goals beyond what he had already achieved.

By the age of fifty-seven, James had become a little too old school for the modern defense contracting business, and corporate management thought it might be a good time for him to think about relinquishing the reins of president. After much prodding, in August 2005, he named a successor, and after further prodding, he announced that he would retire at the end of 2006. Two months later, James went to Washington, D.C., to celebrate the 230th birthday of the U.S. Marines. He failed to attend a precelebration lunch with colleagues and was found dead in his hotel room a few hours later. His death was completely unexpected by all who knew him. No cause of death was determined, and no autopsy was performed. Some presumed suicide, but that is speculation.

It could be that James felt that the orderly life built of choices made three decades earlier was about to be amputated. He may have felt terrified at the lack of order and purpose in his life once he was separated from the routines and responsibilities of his former busy life. Although James never overtly complained, his life with Sarah had become more obligatory than voluntary. In fact, James had stopped making choices two decades earlier. His work was obligatory as well.

It was not in his nature to demand time for himself to pursue new interests, and he came to regard nonessential engagements as frivolous. He napped instead. After years of ignoring the impulse to try new things, to accept invitations to join others in friendship or sports, or even to rethink career options, he had found that the instinct and the invitations stopped completely. He was lonely and bored and not self-aware enough to recognize that he had slipped into a serious depression.

James's angst and his response to it may seem extreme, but not difficult to understand. His slide into the neck of the hourglass was gradual. The most insidious part of getting stuck is that it happens very slowly at first. Almost imperceptibly, the sense of expectancy and hope fades away. Opportunities seem less engaging, and inertia seems inevitable. The notion of waiting for our future to happen subtly replaces the more youthful energy of the future waiting for us.

Jonah tells a story that is different from Quick's or James's on the face of it. He and his partner of thirty years, Meg, gave more thought to their future than did most people their age and began their plans many years earlier. They had chosen not to have kids and had planned their finances carefully. They lived comfortably, but not extravagantly, in Chicago and maintained a cabin in Wisconsin they used in the summers. They intended to retire to Wisconsin, where Meg's parents and siblings lived.

Meg owned a bookstore in downtown Chicago, and Jonah was an independent consultant. They enjoyed each other's company for decades—and the routine that allowed them a city life and a country one. But things began to change as they turned fifty. Jonah felt restless and really lost interest in his business, and for Meg, the David-and-Goliath game she played with the big retailers had lost its charm. They decided to sell her store and the house in Chicago and move to Wisconsin. They were making choices—so far, so good.

At first, they focused their energy on building a new house on the site near their old cabin. They had a wonderful time planning and executing their dream home. They felt new excitement—with each other and for their future. They even got a puppy.

Shortly after the house was completed, Jonah's dad became ill—and so did Meg's mom. Within several months of each other, both died. When the initial grieving period passed, it became clear that because of a variety of circumstances, Meg and Jonah were responsible for their remaining parents—a responsibility they took on willingly, happy to have the time and ability to do so. In Meg's case, this involved daily visits to her father—it had become clear that he suffered from early Alzheimer's. But fortunately, he lived nearby in Wisconsin, as did several siblings, with whom she could share the burden.

Jonah's mom was physically well and determined to be independent, but understandably needed a lot of support in the year that followed her husband's death. Jonah visited her in Chicago weekly.

A year of adjustment came and went—then another and another. In the space of three years, Jonah and Meg had been transformed from a lively urban couple with independent interests and friends—twice-yearly travel, stacks of books to be consumed, and a regular social schedule that included business associates and family—to something else entirely.

The fabric of their lives had changed in a direction they had not anticipated. Their daily routine involved nothing that challenged them or provided a sense of satisfaction. And although they had always thought of themselves as loners, suddenly they felt lonely. They missed the acquaintances and associates that peopled their city life. They felt trapped: trapped by their caretaker responsibilities, trapped by their geographic isolation, and trapped in a relationship that now seemed to have more problems than they had realized.

Although Jonah and Meg had made some significant changes in their fifties, they were trapped in the neck of the hourglass. Perhaps because they had no children, they were unaware of the constraints of caregiving. And most significantly, the choices they made in leaving Chicago limited their options in many other ways. The companionship of others and the engagement of work and social demands had provided a texture to their lives—a texture that they took for granted. In their attempt to simplify their lives and give back to the families they loved, they found themselves mired in a confusing set of "no exits" they had never encountered before.

Jeff: What was completely unexpected is that they became trapped through the conscious choice to do what they thought was right. They didn't see it as a life-changing sacrifice; they just thought it was the right thing to do.

Paula: In a sense, that's what makes their story so significant in exploring the Hourglass Effect. We don't get stuck because we want to. And it's not always because we made bad decisions. Stuck is so very often an unanticipated consequence of doing all the *right* things.

Jeff: Doing all the right things for others but losing one's own sense of direction—it happened to Liz in an entirely different context.

Liz married late, according to her mother. She was, in her own words, "a careerist," having attended Smith College in the late 1970s. Nobody ever called her shy or retiring. She majored in computer science and got a PhD at Stanford, where she was one of very few women in her program. She was actively recruited by corporations up and down both coasts.

She ended up at a software company, where after some initial difficulties, she rose through the ranks and was being groomed to take over as chief technology officer. There she met Bill, who was president of the company and already married—which was actually fine with Liz. An affair suited her. "I didn't have time for a husband," she told us. "I spent most weekends and holidays at the office, and I was glad he could spend that time with his wife so that I didn't have to feel guilty. I think that's probably the opposite of how most women feel. Bill was more demanding about the relationship than I was."

After five years of this very comfortable arrangement—Liz was thirty-four and Bill forty-two—they decided to "get serious" and plan for the future. Bill got divorced; they got married and set about building a family. She was thirty-six when she had her first baby and forty when she had her second. They were overjoyed and overwhelmed. They hired a nanny so that they could continue to work at their former pace, because, as competitive as they were, neither was going to be the one to voluntarily become a stay-at-home parent. But it just wasn't working. "Rationally, it was a simple decision. Bill made more money than I did. So I quit my job in order to 'launch the kids.'"

"It was only going to be for a few years, but one thing just led to another—there was always a problem that I felt I could manage better if I gave it my full attention. And I think that everyone was happier with me at home."

It turned out that "everyone" did not include Liz. "I knew I was sacrificing my career. But Bill talked about the company with me, so I still felt involved in the business world. I don't know how, but a few years became ten. And now it's fourteen. Going back to work stopped making sense a long time ago, but now I don't know what to do with myself. I'm MIA—I don't even remember who I was—why would anyone else?"

Liz has lost her sense of self. In the process of serving her family, she lost the habit of exploration and the joy of achievement. Although her family is a great source of pride and satisfaction, she admits that their accomplishments have become "a little too important" to her. She told us about the extreme disappointment she felt about her son's rejection from a prestigious school.

"I felt like I needed a win. It's been a long time since I had one," she said wistfully. Liz has lost the ability to focus on herself and her own future. "I don't even know what I want anymore—'we' has eaten 'me.'"

What James, Quick, Jonah, Meg, and Liz all have in common is that they found themselves in their fifties thinking that they had few choices for their future. Liz and Meg admit to feeling somewhat depressed and anxious. Both have put on weight and spend far less time and money taking care of themselves than they did a decade ago. Quick drinks too much. Jonah spends hours locked in his study, working at his computer. He feels angry and irritable, and the smallest interruption is likely to provoke an outburst. Meg says he is losing his hearing. Jonah says "maybe so," but refuses to do anything about it.

> **Jeff:** We will discuss work more completely in Chapter 6, but it's worth mentioning that change in work status played a role for everyone in these stories. For Quick and Jonah, it was decreased satisfaction with their work; Meg and Liz made voluntary moves out of the workforce; James was retiring. None of them experienced the euphoria or eager anticipation that might have accompanied an anticipated release from the daily grind. Not even quiet relief.
>
> **Paula:** Their relationships with their partners changed as well. Some confided that they had considered splitting from their spouses, but didn't. Quick did make the split, but didn't become any happier. In Chapter 4, we will focus exclusively on relationships in midlife.

Jeff: There is no one-size-fits-all solution, that's for sure, but there are consistent themes. The one common piece is that everyone who is stuck seems to have lost track of what he or she wants—or what is wanted has changed since the person made decisions long ago.

Although boomers have often been criticized for their narcissism, ironically, many have lost sight of their own goals along the way. They focused on work, partners, and their kids. For previous generations, religion and the social norms that support family and community provided context and meaning, but for boomers, loss of self means loss of their center of gravity.

The crisis of meaning in life is not a new phenomenon, and boomers are not the first generation to face this issue. But boomers are asking themselves these questions much earlier in life than have previous generations and are looking for unique answers that match their distinctive history and path of individual growth.

Boomers are not satisfied with the traditional answers—which are often based on religious dogma or the notion that children offer the key to immortality. They are looking for a more personal resolution to their internal crisis of meaning.

Classic psychological theories of all schools (and particularly the work of Erik Erikson) identify significant developmental life stages.[2] Major transitions are marked by the successful resolution of a psychosocial crisis, which permits further personal growth and progress to the next level. Movement through each stage of development—from child to adolescent, from adolescent to young adult, from young adult to mature adult—requires the achievement of a psychological balance in life. Consciously or not, that balance requires a focus on oneself.

A child's transition from one stage to the next is different in context from that of an adult, but the process is essentially the same and merits the same consideration and respect. The transition to Greater Adulthood involves a consistent and conscientious effort to act as an advocate for oneself. It is a process of self-discovery that builds on the experiences and accomplishments of one's life, but is not wholly defined by the past. It is not about backtracking, nor is it about returning to or recreating our youth. It is about finding new pathways that will free us of patterns we might have once assumed were hardwired. In this stage, we try to acknowledge that some things worked out and others didn't and make sense of the totality of our experiences. Inevitably, we are not pleased with every outcome and may not, in retrospect, see all choices as rational or even within our control, but in this phase, we can look back and knit together our range of experience into a whole cloth. It is energizing and frightening. It is liberating and confusing. It may require challenging many of the ideas—and virtues—associated with being an adult.

> **Paula:** The first challenge is to separate a bit from others around you and to focus on *you*. It's hard to do, because our culture calls this selfish—and narcissism has such a bad rap. But the need—and the right—to focus on yourself may just be the most important epiphany you will ever have for this life stage.

Jeff: Working through the bottleneck and stak-
ing claim to Greater Adulthood involves sorting
through major existential issues such as meaning
and mortality and the smaller personal concerns
that shape our daily priorities.

Paula: It's as if we need a self-knowledge tune-
up. And that is a very personal and private matter.

Jeff: It's not regressive self-absorption; it is
taking stock of where the decisions, good and
bad, of the last twenty years have positioned you
on your life map.

This transition begins with permission to think about life
differently. Some find help from friends or partners, but inevitably, the most important permission comes from oneself. In
your adult life, you have experienced much that you are proud
of. This is an important part of the self-audit. But you must
also assess what got lost along the way. It is difficult work, but
an essential preparation for the next life stage.

Some boomers will continue to postpone or ignore these
issues, but for most people, the step into their fifties will require some immediate attention. They will need to reevaluate
their goals and accomplishments. They will need to examine
their relationships and their expectations and the responsibilities inherent in those relationships. They will also need to
again balance the trade-offs between work and money and job
satisfaction. And they will have to address the demands of
their bodies. This is not the first time, and it may not be the
last, that boomers will take stock of their lives, but the experiences and outcomes of the previous decades can help tailor
these decisions.

The power to emerge from the neck of the hourglass and claim the full range of possibilities that making choices creates is the promise of the Hourglass Solution. In the chapters to come, we will meet men and women who have faced these issues and transformed the quality of their lives.

4

The People in Our Lives: Renovating Relationships

You created the play in which you are now engaged—but after decades in the very specific roles of husband, wife, mother, son, it is difficult to separate the actor from the role. Would you play these characters again? Would you cast the same central players in your life if you could do it all over? One of the first hurdles in creating a personal Hourglass Solution is the people in our lives.

Adult life is a web of entanglements. Relationships are so inextricably bound up with identity, it is hard to even contemplate personal change without considering the enormous impact it will have on those close to us. The thought of disturbing the delicate balance finally achieved in those relationships is unsettling. For some, it is simply too terrifying.

Although relationships can be constraints in creating a new lifescape, the strong ones flourish all the more through renovation. The first step takes courage. It requires that we analyze the ties that bind us to the people in our lives, and evaluate the merits of each one, in the present, and for our future.

This chapter is a guide to looking at intimate relationships, evaluating them, and understanding how to create options even when there appear to be none. Making choices and effecting change in the most personal sphere of life is the heart of an Hourglass Solution.

Your People Universe

The universe of people who are important in our lives is a function of our chronological age, personality characteristics, personal history, and cultural environment. Consider for a moment the magnitude of differences from the associations of tribal society to the relationships linked through Facebook. The number of connections, the quality of the interaction, and their importance to us are all factors in the topography of our people universe.

It changes throughout our lifetime, but by the time we reach our fifties, the people universe we live in is well mapped and, relative to other life stages, reasonably stable. For boomers, it is likely to be more diverse than it was for previous generations, but is perhaps smaller than that of their children. In 2000, the U.S. Census identified twenty-one relationship codes within a single household unit, which resulted in 786,000 possible household combinations, as opposed to a fraction of those recognized in 1950.[1] Today, as many as five generations live in a single household, as well as in-laws, unmarried significant others, children by previous relationships, half-siblings, nonrelatives—and the list goes on. This is just one measure of the diversity of relationship configurations enjoyed by boomers. A statistical snapshot reveals some other interesting boomer patterns:

- Highest divorce rate (36 percent of boomers have ever been divorced, versus 16 percent for those aged sixty-five and over)

- Highest percentage of people never married (15 percent, versus 4 percent for those aged sixty-five and over)

- Highest number of unmarried couples living together (twelvefold increase from 1960 to 2000)

- Least likely to have children (30 percent never had children, versus 20 percent of those age sixty-five and over)

- Most likely to have their parents still living (27 percent of fifty-year-olds today have both parents living, versus 14 percent of fifty-year-olds in 1960)[2]

For most of us, our people universe includes blood relatives, stepfamilies, partners, ex-spouses, close friends, and associates who occupy different amounts of our psychic energy and space. It is populated by intimate relationships, which elicit intense emotions, and includes the people whom we see every day at work and in our communities and with whom we maintain defined boundaries, regardless of our fondness for them.

The family members we see, and those we don't, arrange themselves in time and space that can reflect affection but often is about geography. Friends are, for some of us, the most important constellation in our universe. For others, they are peripheral to relationships that are more primary. The characters in our lives are diverse. They fulfill different roles, and we learn to count on them for different things.

What about our own roles? Some people always take center stage. They are the leader of their social group and the center of a family circle. They are the organizer of events, holiday celebrations, reunions, and vacations. Others have chosen the reluctant and long-suffering role, but are reliably present for any occasion. Still others prefer not to interact with groups of any kind and restrict their involvements to one-on-ones. Some people are entertainers. Others are the necessary audience. Although there is enormous range on this dimension, we have found that for the most part, people are consistent. They play the same role, adjusted for circumstance, across numerous venues. For some, this has been true since childhood. For others, consistency has come only with time, as specific roles have proved to be more effective or at least comfortable at work, at home, and with friends. Some people are practiced chameleons who can readily become what the situation requires.

> **Paula:** The question now is, how satisfying are the roles you have been playing? Does the work of being the center of your family circle make you feel generous and appreciated or just worn out? Do you like being the one who always calls first to plan a movie or dinner, or do you want your friends to take more initiative now and then?
>
> **Jeff:** Is the role you think you play really an accurate description now—or are you toting around some outmoded assumptions about yourself? The intact nuclear family is a historical relic, but

boomers haven't abandoned family completely as some pundits of the 1960s predicted. But boomers have redefined it.

Paula: Whatever relationships comprise your people universe, the question to be resolved is this: Are the choices you made earlier in your life still relevant? Are your relationships still working for you in the manner in which you had hoped? And most importantly, what are the options for your next life stage?

No amount of self-awareness grants a do-over. Remediation in life is about moving forward. The point of looking at your relationships is not to discard them. That is a separate decision you may want to undertake at another time. For now, the point is to figure out what is working and what isn't. Sometimes, the cast and characters are all the more loveable after years of wear, but the roles have gotten tired.

Often without meaning to do so, other people contribute to the feeling of our being stuck in a life that is no longer of our choosing. Recrimination and blame are proven nonstarters. Self-awareness and examination could help uncover some vestigial habits and practices.

Jeff: In this chapter, we will raise questions about the major relationships in our lives from the perspective of choice and control.

Paula: There are more options than you may be aware of. By identifying other possibilities, you gain control.

Family

Some people are irrevocably "family people." They have been involved with parents and children and brothers and sisters and aunts and uncles and cousins for decades. Someone is the glue that holds it together. Someone provides "comic relief." Someone is the family therapist. Someone is the chief organizer. Whatever role you play in your extended family, emotionally and functionally, you've probably been playing it for many years. Take some time to look at how it is going for you *now*. Is this a part you still want to play, or is there another format that would suit you better?

Making Choices

Anne is a wife and a mother of five children. She took care of her own mother and her in-laws through their old age and various illnesses and is a deacon in her church. Anne is at the center of everything "family." Her table always expands to include the great-aunt or distant cousin, the spouses of her own children and sometimes their in-laws, and, more recently, a gaggle of grandchildren. Family has been her life, and she is understandably proud and increasingly tired.

Jonathan is one of four brothers and professionally the most successful by a wide margin. For the last thirteen years, he and his partner, Stephen, have hosted the brothers and their families for a three-day gala Christmas celebration in New York City. The event always includes at least one Broadway show and dinners at expensive restaurants. Jon and Stephen plan every detail and pick up the full tab.

Marilou and her husband have worked tirelessly at creating a blended family. They each brought two children to their marriage and, for fifteen years, took every opportunity to create inclusive and interesting occasions for their four kids and, eventually, the kids' significant others. It required patience and continual adjustments to accommodate the demands of their exes, the in-laws, and geography. They were determined to create a warm and supportive environment for everyone. And against all odds, they did so for many years.

Anne, Jonathan, and Marilou are the lucky winners of the family lottery. They have defined themselves as family people and have been very successful in nurturing those around them. They have suffered disappointments, like everyone else, but what distinguishes them from so many others is that their unflagging commitment to a family ideal has sustained them—until now.

Anne has suffered from many debilitating, though thankfully non-life-threatening, illnesses in the last few years. With a part-time job, two daughters who are pregnant, and two more with endless babysitting needs, she is simply out of gas. "When I hear the phone ring, I don't want to say hello; I just want to say no!" she told us, "but I'm not comfortable with that."

Although Jon and Stephen have enjoyed being hosts, they have begun to resent it. "It's just that it has become so expected. I don't think anyone is even grateful anymore."

Marilou still has energy, but is tired of compromising. She feels that she has earned the right to have just a few holidays "exactly as I want them." "I don't want to share Thanksgiving or celebrate Christmas on the twenty-sixth. I want it my way—at least once."

Anne, Jon, and Marilou are stuck. Although they have played their family roles successfully, it has become tiresome. They feel mired in a seemingly endless series of chores and compromises that are expected, but not necessarily appreciated. The roles they chose to play *in* their family and *for* their family were important parts of their identity for many years, but the accumulated resentment is straining relationships for all of them. All three of them have reaped the rewards of a commitment made to family early in their adulthood, but these commitments now feel more like unmitigated obligation.

We heard family stories like Anne's, Jon's, and Marilou's dozens of times in one form or another. In most cases, we found that the patterns, not the people, were the problem. Patterns of a lifetime were no longer satisfying rituals, but, rather, paralyzing ones.

Happily, each of these three adults was able to understand what part of the family routine had become disabling and to make modifications. Jon decided to take a breather from his family holidays, opting instead to vacation alone with Stephen in a warm climate. Anne and Marilou, through open dialogue with their husbands and kids, modified their roles in family activities.

Holidays are not the only time when family expectations and demands collide with one's ability for choice and personal gratification, but they can provide a useful lens for identifying patterns that are embedded in other aspects of the relationship. Making choices about long-standing family arrangements may, at the very least, provide some refreshment of relationships that have been in need of change. The choices may also play a pivotal role in setting one free of the patterns that have stopped being valuable. Most important is the exercise of personal prerogative and control in an arena that probably has more options than you may have thought.

Partners and Spouses

Baby boomers have had an uneasy relationship with the institution of marriage, and yet 65 percent of boomers are currently married and an estimated 10 percent more are living with a significant other.[3] These partnerships can contribute to the feeling of being stuck in the hourglass or can be an accelerator for breaking out.

In long-term relationships, couples build a shared life, with all its positive and negative aspects. Couples are also complicit in erecting walls to protect decisions already taken.

The big choices, as well as the little ones, define who we are as couples. Choices made provide the glue to our relationships, but they are also the gummy sludge that holds us in the neck of the hourglass. Midlife is an appropriate juncture to revisit some of the choices we have made over the years. Part of the exercise is exposure: Some of the choices we have made as couples are no longer visible to us. We have been behaving in the same way for so long, we no longer realize that we have alternatives.

Couples have a sense of what they are together—their "couple identity." Cultivated over the years, it can include everything from where they live and the way they look, to the other people they enjoy being with and the things they like to do together. Some parts of a couple identity remain constant through the years, but sometimes, aspects of the old identity are no longer satisfying or useful and are simply constraining.

The Hourglass Solution requires that we accept the idea that we have made choices about who we are as a couple and that these decisions are subject to change. We chose who we were and have control over who we will become in the future.

> **Paula:** Philip and I saw ourselves as an urban couple. We have always been city people—until we realized that we weren't anymore. We didn't work in the city, and most of our friends had moved elsewhere. That's when we started to think about moving. It was very liberating. The old identity just took up psychic space, like old clothes that are never worn, occupying valuable closet real estate.
>
> **Jeff:** It is important to discuss with your partner who you want to be in your next incarnation. Like all the other couple transition stages you have probably gone through, this next one is dynamic and ongoing. It is a work in process—at least it is for us. I thought we were "done" after the third time we moved.
>
> **Paula:** I remember asking Phil once, quite some time ago, what he thought we'd be like when we were seventy. He said, "Very thin and very tan." It started as a joke. It became a kind of iconic fantasy, but was the beginning of a dialogue that is ongoing.
>
> **Jeff:** It can be very helpful to have a mental picture of where your future is headed—like seeing pictures of a vacation spot you are looking forward to.

Creating meaningful choices begins with knowing what *you* want. Then the negotiations with your partner can begin.

Compromises, accommodations, and manipulations allow two people to live together peacefully, but confronting transitions poses some unique difficulties. Change can be threatening to couple identity, and inevitably, people's appetite for change and the timing of changes will differ as well. Although some of the boomers we spoke with found no solution other than divorce, separation, or a tacitly agreed-upon marital truce, most found that the process of moving through the neck of the hourglass actually provided immense opportunity to revitalize their relationships.

Couples confronting the neck of the hourglass can help or hinder the process for each other. You can facilitate or abort self-discovery for your partner. Perhaps you think you would change some things in your life if it were not for your spouse, who insists that things stay in place:

"I'd chuck it all and move someplace else tomorrow. But Mary won't even discuss it."

"I'm so bored with all our friends. But Charles is perfectly content listening to the same stupid stories."

"I'm optimistic but Jewel—I think she's a little afraid of the future."

"I am still young—but Sam isn't."

This is the couple vocabulary in the language of stuck. No doubt there are some real barriers to change, but generally there are far fewer than it first appears. The important thing is to realize that over the years, couples develop patterns that may have been functional at some point but can also contribute to being stuck. One partner is the spender, and the other is a saver. One is the social butterfly; the other is less so. One most often initiates new activities; the other reliably puts on the brakes. Whatever the pattern, you have worked with it, and around it, for many years. It is likely that questioning basic couple assumptions and long-standing behavior will be uncomfortable at first, but the alternative of submitting to constraints that no longer serve you well is equally uncomfortable.

Jeff: Sometimes, patterns are set by situations that no longer exist. In my relationship, it took a while for me to see this. When I had a more demanding career than Hyrum, it was my job that dictated where we lived, when we took vacations, and whether we had enough money to buy a new car. Over the years, his career took off, but we didn't change the patterns we had established. We were living in Atlanta because of my job, which I no longer enjoyed. And Hyrum was commuting every week to New York, coming home exhausted on Friday night. He thought that we should move to New York and that I should be the one to change jobs. In retrospect, it was blindingly obvious—just not to me. I'd never played that role before. When Hyrum first suggested it, I could hardly hear him, but he kept at it until I did. It literally changed our lives.

Paula: Even a small shift in attitude can create new solutions. If you are the naysayer in the relationship—try to loosen up a bit. If you are the risk taker—try to pull back just enough to reassure your partner without giving up completely.

Jeff: For us, deliberately changing some of the power dynamics was fun. We all get so used to the roles we play in our primary relationships that we can lose sight of whether we still enjoy them.

Paula: Perhaps your partner is waiting for a stepped-down plan that could work for both of you. The only unacceptable stance is to do nothing. Couples need to push each other a bit.

Jeff: Look at your life, and talk with your partner. You don't need to fix it all at once. Fix one thing—anything. Paint a room, clean a closet. Talk about it as a metaphor for change.

Couple relationships invariably involve friends, who, in our people universe, are constellations that change throughout our lives. Couples learn to accommodate differences in their needs for friendships and create diverse social arrangements that include *his* friends, *her* friends, and *our* friends. At different times, friendships perform different functions, and the transition to Greater Adulthood is no exception. We need our friends to be part of the solution, because they can help us identify new choices and to help us with the stresses that are an inevitable part of change. Without friends, our primary relationship carries the full burden of stimulation and feedback. Boomers have intuitively known that one person is unlikely to fulfill all needs, and this is no time to forget that. It is unreasonable to expect a spouse or significant other to provide all the identity reinforcement and feedback that once came from a job.

Arden tells of her difficult adjustment to the retirement of her husband, a former chief economist who is now writing a book about his experiences in the global investment-banking business. "Ben was used to having an entire *battalion* of people who thought he was brilliant—or at least acted as if they did. If he had an idea, twenty people swore it was 'important,' and twenty more dug up the facts to support it. Then one of his three secretaries would type it up and distribute it to his 'select' monthly mailing list. Now, he expects me to listen to every sentence and applaud enthusiastically. Then he wants to know what's for lunch. I don't know what happened to my life."

Ben expresses the other side of the issue poignantly. "It's not that I miss anyone in particular, but I am used to having lots of people around who, I guess just by their presence, affirm something about me to me. From my group of colleagues, I know that I am funny, smart, and astute about politics, an opinion leader—valued for my diverse experiences. I just don't get that from my wife."

The expectation that Arden can provide the kind of support that an entire company gave Ben before his retirement is unrealistic. But there are other sources of feedback.

Cynthia and Bill get essential feedback by going out once a week—with a friend and *without each other*. "When Bill was younger, he traveled a lot," says Cynthia. "I used that time to see friends on my own—to get out a bit and keep my sanity. And it was great to be 'just me'—not part of a couple in a social environment. When he stopped traveling, I stopped 'dating' until I realized how much I missed it! We spend so much more time together now, I think it's even more important than before."

Jeff: The need to go out on your own and maintain independent friendships is important for many reasons. It presents you with feedback on yourself—not just as part of a couple. It also provides you the opportunity to give voice to things you have been thinking but perhaps don't want to share with your partner. Maybe your partner has different political views and, after all these years, you are tired of arguing with him. But that doesn't mean that others aren't interested in what you have to say.

Paula: One of the great joys of easing up on the work schedule of early adulthood is spending more time with your significant other. But there can be too much of a good thing. Don't think of "dating" someone else as times stolen from your partner. Think of it as giving your loved one necessary relief. You will come home refreshed—and with something new to talk about.

Jeff: This isn't so easy for a lot of people. We heard a lot of pushback from the people we talked to, and it sounded like this:

"Joe would just sit by the phone and worry."

"Ellen would have a fit—for sure, she'd think I was having an affair."

"Yes, but John really doesn't like it when I go out without him. He doesn't know what to do with himself."

Paula: "Yes, but . . ." is the language of stuck. If it sounds like a good idea to you, take the time and effort to make your partner understand that time with other people doesn't mean he or she is less important.

Jeff: Friends who make the cut should be cherished. Friends are the witnesses to our lives. They

help us define who we are. And they help us remember who we are, because they hold us to the
standard we have set for ourselves. Maintaining
relationships through life transitions can be challenging, but neglecting these relationships is a
dangerous risk.

    Paula: Do so at your own peril. If you are com-
mitted to a full and adventurous life, don't lose
touch with the people who could help make that
possible.

If you are a people person, social engagement is your
lifeblood. For some of us, work provided the network beyond
family life, but as it winds down, we can't get lazy about keeping relationships. They are more important than they may have
appeared. These relationships give us important feedback and
new information on who we are and who we are becoming. It
is unfair and unrealistic to expect a spouse to do all that heavy
lifting, even if the spouse thinks he or she can do it or should
be doing it. People who need people need to assert their right
to do so.

Uncoupling

Most of the couples we talked with were able to sort out an
Hourglass Solution together—even those who were clearly going through a rough patch. Inevitably, this will not be true for
everyone. Uncoupling is, for some, a necessary part of moving
into Greater Adulthood. The process of separation and divorce
is never pleasant, but it can also be liberating.

David Popenoe, who heads the National Marriage Project at Rutgers University, weighs in on the issue of uncoupling: "The decline in marriage is due to secular individualism . . . a preoccupation with personal autonomy and self-fulfillment and a political emphasis on egalitarianism and the tolerance of diverse lifestyles."[4]

> **Jeff:** Personal autonomy and self-fulfillment aren't necessarily incompatible with marriage, but if marriage seriously inhibits autonomy and is a barrier to self-fulfillment, then divorce should be an option.
>
> **Paula:** Egalitarianism within marriage is a stressful negotiation for boomers, most of whom were raised in homes where gender-linked division of labor was the norm. Women who have struggled for equality in their lives outside the home are hardly likely to give it up to a husband.
>
> **Jeff:** Sounds like a deal breaker to me.
>
> **Paula:** When I was a kid in the suburbs in the 1950s, I only knew one divorced family. The difficulties the kids faced and the isolation the parents experienced are hardly imaginable now. Divorce, while never pleasant, has to be an option for couples who find that new choices led them in incompatible directions.
>
> **Jeff:** So, for couples in midlife who find that their relationship is an insuperable obstacle to finding Greater Adulthood, divorce may be a reasonable, if not totally positive, choice.

Martha was studying theatrical costume design at Indiana University when she met her future husband, Frank, who was getting his degree in set design. After they graduated, they thought it would be impossible to find a place where both of them could get jobs. But as Martha said, "The god of theater smiled on us, and two jobs opened up simultaneously at a wonderful small college in New Hampshire."

For twenty-five years, they worked at the college. "At first, of course, it was wonderful," Martha told us. "It was what we had both studied for. But after a while, it got to be too much. Every year, new students came in, and we'd do another production of *Death of a Salesman* or *Our Town* or *Cabaret.*"

Some years, Martha was fed up and wanted to leave; some years, it was Frank who had had enough. But they stuck it out for the students, themselves, and each other. As both Martha and Frank admitted, they were on autopilot.

When Martha broke her hand in 2002, it was the catalyst that got things moving. "I couldn't sew twenty costumes in a week, so I had to hire an assistant. And, you know, everything was fine. The show went on. And it dawned on me that I was not the indispensable pillar of the theater. They could live without me, and it would be just fine."

Long talks with Frank ensued, and they realized that they both felt stuck. Martha had longed to leave the small New England town for a bigger city and start a wedding-dress business. Frank wanted to stay in town, but design kitchens and bathrooms instead of theater sets. Martha knew she could build her business anywhere because of all her connections with former students. Frank knew he needed to stay in Lawrenceville.

So, after twenty-six years of marriage, they divorced. Neither Frank nor Martha would say they've "never been happier"—they had lived through many, many wonderful times together. But they both agree that they would not be nearly as happy today if they were still married, still living together in the small New England town, still working in the college theater, still living on autopilot. For them, divorce was a prerequisite for getting their lives moving again.

> **Paula:** They are interesting because it doesn't sound as if they were angry. Nor does it seem that they faced a deal-breaker issue that they couldn't get over. They were quietly miserable, not enjoying each other and dreaming secret dreams.
>
> **Jeff:** They had become diminished people—a case where one plus one was equaling way less then two.
>
> **Paula:** The hopeful point is that they were able to realize they were holding each other back from something much more exciting.
>
> **Jeff:** Last time we checked, Martha's bridal business was thriving and she was enjoying her bigger life. Frank has been dating a woman he has known for years, and they have begun to discuss their future together.

Uncoupling is sometimes not a choice. There are over 14 million widows and widowers in the United States and over 800,000 new ones each year.[5]

Joanna found a very different "me" after the death of her husband. For more than three years, she had dedicated herself to his care. Her only time off was spent ministering to her still-young children. In an almost unimaginable pile-on of catastrophe, her stepson was tragically killed in the same period. Joanna steadfastly managed her husband's failing health, the loss of his child, and the everyday lives of their three younger kids. Not surprisingly, her friends called her Saint Jo. It would have been easy to understand if after her husband died, she had wanted to rest and retreat from the world for a while, but that is not what happened.

"After Bart died, I had an enormous desire for change. I wanted to travel—and I wanted to move. I took three trips in six months, and then I started to look for a new home. It was good that I looked, but I realized that maybe moving wasn't a great idea. I still wanted to change *something,* though. So I redecorated our bedroom and got three dogs! Crazy, huh?"

But that isn't all she did. Her husband's illness involved many emergencies and much nursing care, which she managed—hands-on and intimately. After he died, she decided that some good must come of all this experience, so she trained for and became certified as an emergency medical technician (EMT). Today, she serves her community as part of the EMT team—and when Hurricane Katrina hit in 2005, she volunteered to be part of emergency relief.

Joanna's experience with illness and death actually helped her to discover a part of herself that has been evolving ever since. She learned that she is, instinctively, a caregiver. She does it exceptionally well—and joyously. She has found ways to take that knowledge and build and develop it. It has made her choices clearer and her ability to help others more focused as well.

"I enjoy helping people. And I know I do it well. But I do it on my terms—I will not be taken advantage of. That was a hard one for me to learn."

One is struck by Joanna's "lightness" these days. It is easy to make her laugh—at a good joke or at herself. Someone who has known her a long time told us recently, "Jo is more Jo than ever."

Martha and Frank chose to start new lives. Joanna's journey was involuntary. For all three, it was through their pain that they learned to focus on themselves. And that focus has given them access to their adult identity.

The relationship with a spouse or life partner is a defining one. It can help us squeeze through the neck of the hourglass, or it can keep us stuck. But we found that more times than not, the journey revitalizes this most important relationship.

What If There Is No "We"?

Twenty-five percent of boomers currently live alone. There are many variations of this story: Some never married, some are widowed or divorced, some have chosen a single life, and some have settled for it. Societal tolerance of untraditional alternatives has been liberating for some, but for others, it has led to an indefinite stalling period. Freedom from the constraints of partnering has provided many boomers with the dividends of personal autonomy. Many have chosen to pursue an agenda unfettered by the needs of others and have risen to prominence in the arts, science, and industry—while others continue to search for the perfect partner who can be the singular witness to their lives. Some say they just like living alone and making their own decisions.

Never before have so many adults lived on their own. Boomers redefined this demographic segment and expanded the old stereotypes from spinster to the women of *Sex and the City*.

Bachelorhood, as well, became more acceptable and nuanced. "Single by choice" or "failure to launch"—the phenomenon is as much part of our generation's story as sex, drugs, and rock and roll. Some argue that the phenomenon is a consequence. Whatever the cause, it is a familiar story with many variations.

Without the wake-up calls of marker events such as empty nests and double-digit wedding anniversaries, midlife can be especially confusing for singles. Practiced in the habit of autonomous choices, many single people find themselves cast in tiresome roles by others in their people universe. In Stephen Sondheim's musical *Company*, the perennially single man, Robert, fulfills the needs of his many married friends by providing them with whatever is missing in their marriages. "What would we do without you? How would we ever get through?" they ask their friend and enumerate the many roles he plays in their lives. Although Robert is indispensable to their lives, we wonder if they are indispensable to his.

Like the relationship bottleneck experienced by couples, single people often fall into patterns that they chose long ago with friends and family. The favorite uncle may have gotten tired of his command performances.

"I adore my sister," Scott told us, "and I don't want to hurt her feelings. But I don't have kids of my own, and I'm sick of all the dinners and soccer games and endless piano recitals. Maybe it's just too much of a good thing, but I would like to take some time off from my family. I wouldn't mind missing a few celebrations. They act as though just because I'm not doing the cooking, I'm not doing much—that really isn't fair."

Jeff: Singles have a big advantage in defining an Hourglass Solution in that they don't need to

negotiate change with a partner—making independent choices is their habit.

Paula: The converse is that they don't always
have a built-in support system or source of feedback to help them get through it. I think this is
what many singles lack—someone to tell them
when they're being an ass. Friends aren't always so
frank.

Jeff: The issue is the same for all of us: Are
your relationships enabling choices, or do they increasingly feel like a series of obligations? Scott is
stuck in obligation and is feeling more and more
resentful.

Paula: We also met many singles who were
able to make life-expanding choices because they
had fewer obligations.

Jeff: I went to high school with a Norwegian
kid named Mathias who wanted to be a professional musician. Since he played accordion, that
did not seem like a promising possibility.

After he graduated from the University of Washington,
Mathias got a job on a cruise ship, strolling through the din-
ing room, playing accordion during dinner. He has been doing that ever since—about thirty years. Mathias loves his
job. He has seen every corner of the world accessible by
cruise ship. He has made friends with fellow musicians
around the globe and visits them regularly. Recently, he
played with a chamber music group in Vienna for a month
between cruise jobs, since over the years, he has also learned
to play piano.

When we last spoke, the subject of marriage came up and I asked him if that was in the cards. He said he hadn't the inclination. "You have to make too many compromises. If you marry someone who isn't in the cruise business, then you're apart for ten months out of the year. So what's the point? And if you marry someone who *is* in the cruise business, you don't always get the best trips, because you need two job openings instead of just one. Two good friends of mine are ship singers, and they sail half the year in the Caribbean and half the year in Alaska—seeing the same ports over and over and over again. Me? Last year, I sailed off South America, in the Mediterranean, and in the Baltic. I even went to Antarctica."

"I'm extremely lucky," he told us. "I can keep doing this until I'm sixty-five or seventy. And the buffet is free."

For some single people, friendships have taken the place of family. For many, that has been nourishing and productive, but for others, it has become problematic. By the age of fifty-three, Joyce, although unmarried, had accumulated an entourage of friends—her best friend, Denise, with whom she shared a house in the Hamptons every summer; and her platonic male friends, who proffered frequent dinner invitations as well as a ready supply of movie and theater opportunities. Joyce's friends seemed like the one constant in a sea of ups and downs.

There was series of major upsets. Her first, early-in-life marriage had ended badly, and Joyce, despite her vocal protests to the contrary, wasn't really interested in getting married again. Then her high-powered job at a major investment bank was phased out. This left her with a substantial severance package, but significantly less personal status than she was accustomed to. At about the same time, Joyce's mother became decidedly frail, both mentally and physically. This put additional pressure on Joyce to care for both parents, as her father had never fended well for himself. But her friends were there by her side as she had always been for them. So far, so good, but something insidious was also happening. Like a spouse who fails to see that her partner has grown unhappy with the constraints of the marriage, Joyce's friends didn't see that her New York life had ceased to nourish her. Her job and her family were an endless source of pressure and obligation. When she tried to share her frustrations with her most intimate friends, they brushed her concerns aside. "Oh, Joyce, you are only happy if you have something to complain about. Besides, it takes years to be on the advance list for the sample sales. You can't give that up." Like the machinations of a massive solar system, Joyce occupied a fixed position in her friends' galaxy. They loved her, but did not see that she needed their support to enable change.

So when one day, Joyce announced that she was selling her apartment in New York and had taken a job at a children's charity in Phoenix, her friends were shocked—to put it mildly. Joyce was, to them, the consummate single, self-absorbed New Yorker. She had never even mentioned that she liked kids. What could she possibly find in Phoenix that she didn't have in New York?

For one thing—new friends.

As Joyce found herself getting caught tighter and tighter in the neck of the hourglass, she knew she had to do something to break out. The relationships in her life had become like a rusted set of gears—immovable. As so often happens, her family and friends had developed such rigid expectations that she couldn't reinvent herself. They expected her to be a high-powered executive with an expensive wardrobe, a witty dinner partner, and a dutiful daughter. They didn't see that she had evolved and that her priorities had changed. The annual pilgrimage to Canyon

Ranch had become much less important—in fact, all the trappings of her life that once enhanced her identity now inhibited the person she felt she was becoming. In her mind, her only choice was to start over—in a new city with new friends.

The relationships in your life can be a significant asset or a major hindrance in helping you craft your Hourglass Solution. In Joyce's case, they held her back and she couldn't see any way out. Moving to a new city, where she could start over with a clean slate of relationships, was her solution—and a viable one. Six months after her move to Phoenix, we asked Joyce if she thought it was the right thing to do. "Banking is really a very superficial industry," she explained. "And I felt like a lot of my relationships were based on superficial things—money, clothes, connections. I just couldn't sort through it all. I had to leave New York and do something completely different. I will probably move back one day. But not for a couple of years. By then, I'll have a much better idea of what *I* want instead of what I think other people want from me. I found it difficult to change my life when the people around me weren't getting it."

Joyce's story is a cautionary tale. For singles, friends are often the most important support system. However, the dynamics of friendship—like everything else—evolves over time. Constructing an Hourglass Solution is hard work for everyone. It requires that we scrutinize our closest relationships: Do they enable or disable our universe of options?

Parents

Although life expectancy has increased most dramatically for boomers, it has also increased for their parents. The result is a generational issue of enormous magnitude. The promise of a long adult relationship with one's parents and the possibility of multigenerational bonds are coupled with the knowledge that, for many, this also means a prolonged period of caregiving. Nearly 40 percent of boomers have at least one unhealthy parent; of this 40 percent, most are providing substantial care.[6]

Caregiving can create considerable strain financially and emotionally.[7] As life expectancy for our parents grows, this often means a prolonged period of dependence on other family members. For some boomers, it means a financial burden equal to that of the children they have just raised.[8] For others, it puts a damper on plans to change jobs or even locations. At minimum, it is confusing and can present an obstacle, real or imagined, to significant redefinition for boomers as they age.

Dean and Kathy have taken on their parental care responsibilities as merely a longitudinal extension of their child-care duties. Kathy teaches sixth grade, and Dean is the manager at a major chain restaurant. As soon as their two kids graduated from college, Kathy's mom was diagnosed with Alzheimer's disease and was forced to enter a nursing care facility. Although he stayed at home, Kathy's dad needed daily care, as well.

As Kathy told us, "We could have kept mom home a little longer, but dad wouldn't let anybody else touch her. We had a nurse come in every single day—but dad yelled at nurses so much that they all refused to come back. I remember one nurse who was trying to give mom a sponge bath. Dad screamed at her, 'That's not how Arlene likes her sponge bath. Do it like this.' I have no idea how dad knew mom's preference in sponge baths. But he was insistent.

"So mom moved to a nursing home, and dad stayed in the apartment. Of course, dad can't cook for himself—he never could. He can't clean for himself, either. He just sits and watches

TV all day long. So Dean and I trade off every day after work. One day, Dean visits my dad and I visit my mom. And the next day, we switch.

"I think we're lucky. Neither mom nor dad lives with us, which would be impossible in our apartment. But both mom and dad live about a half-hour away. And I don't mean this in the wrong way, but Dean's parents are both gone. If we had four parents to take care of, I don't what I'd do."

Neither Dean nor Kathy is unhappy—but they are stuck. Their jobs are on autopilot. They can't even consider changing careers or taking on more responsibility—because they need the flexibility they are currently allowed. And their personal relationship has become static and routine—no vacations, few dinners out, take-out food and a rented movie every night at home as their primary source of entertainment. Dean and Kathy feel that they have no choice.

> **Jeff:** I think the critical point here is how Dean and Kathy defined their options: none. They do what they think is right, but they have derived no satisfaction from it. They say they have no choice, but in fact they do. I suspect they would take pride in the care they are providing if they realized they were doing it not because they "have to," but because they "want to." It is a very different mind-set.
>
> **Paula:** Yes, "I want to do this" gives you ownership. "Have to" is actually quite passive and implies loss of control. I found that with my own parents, once I realized that I wanted to be avail-

able to them—that it was something I was doing because it made me feel happy—I felt no resentment at all. On the contrary, I felt privileged to be able to give them something they needed . . . me.

Jeff: There is often no simple answer—especially when money and time are so scarce for so many boomers. The U.S. Administration on Aging developed a Web site with links to local assistance, which demonstrates how profound the need for help outside the family can be. It is a national problem, not just a personal one.

The so-called sandwich generation (sandwiched between one's not-quite-grown children and one's soon-to-be-dependent parents) faces a crisis of allocation. Ten million boomers are now raising kids or supporting an adult child while also giving financial assistance to an aging parent.[9] If choices aren't made and the momentum of events is the driver, the drain on resources of all kinds can be overwhelming. The responsibility for aging parents changes the emotional dynamics of your people universe. Not only is the dependency role reversed, but a dependent parent is also an unhappy harbinger of the future. There is no universal panacea except to understand that there are always options. A decision that some choices are unacceptable is very different from the assertion that choice is unavailable. The phrase "I have no choice" is a clear signal of a bottleneck. "I made a choice to care for dad at home" has very different emotional consequences. One is a statement of control, and the other is a statement of stuck.

Empty-Nest Syndrome

Boomers had fewer kids per household, but most boomers did have children. Thirty-six million empty-nest households are anticipated by 2026.[10] People who have devoted twenty-plus years to raising children often find it difficult to see themselves in any other role but parent, and yet they must, if they want to move forward. There is much awareness of empty-nest syndrome, but little insight. Everyone knows what it is and when it is scheduled to occur, but there is little consensus on exactly what the parents are expected to do about it.

We found that many parents of adult children had great difficulty making new choices that might have made this empty-nest period an opportunity for revitalization and the launch pad of an Hourglass Solution. The important issue is a review of the parenting relationship—and the ability to shift from caregiver to just caring.

The response to this change in parenting status is not simple. Accepting the adultness of a child, which means accepting his or her separateness, may be as life-altering as the birth of that child. Without this transition, the relationship between parents and children stagnates and, for the parents, becomes another aspect of being stuck in the neck of the hourglass.

Debbie still lives outside Denver, in the suburban home she bought over twenty-five years ago, when she was married and soon to have children. The location was inconvenient for her, since it required an hour and a half commute to her office, but she and her husband thought it was "best for the kids." The couple divorced nearly fifteen years ago, and "the kids" are now twenty-one and eighteen.

Yet the pattern of Debbie's life has changed very little—except that she says she finds it a lot less exciting. "All my friends tell me that I should move into the city. I guess it might actually give me some sort of social life, if that's important at my age. But I do think that kids need a place to come home to if they need it—whenever they need it—and someplace they can bring their friends to. Both of them are going to be in college next year. But they'll still need a place to go on school breaks. And from what I've read, kids sometimes move back in for a while after college. Why not?"

Debbie not only continues to pay all her children's bills, but also manages their free time as well. When we last spoke to her, she was fretting over what the eighteen-year-old would do for the summer. She plans and administers the details of their lives just as she did when they were very little. Unfortunately, no one feels good about it, but they don't seem to be able to identify another alternative.

Debbie's relationship with her children (who are now legal adults) hasn't budged in two decades. They are her dependents in every imaginable way, and Debbie is stuck in the neck of the hourglass. She can't move, because of "the kids." She can't quit her job, which she has grown to hate, because she needs the money to support "the kids." Her relationships with friends and the possibilities for dating are equally curtailed.

Debbie tells us she has no options.

Harold and Betty have often thought about downsizing and moving to another part of the country. They could just about swing it with the proceeds from their sprawling colonial, whose value (as of 2007, when we spoke with them) had escalated quite handsomely. But Harold continues to work at a job ("just for the money") that he has lost heart for since it became clear he would never become CEO.

They decided they needed to postpone their decision to start a new life because their two daughters, aged twenty-five and twenty-eight, are not yet married and, in Harold and Betty's minds, are "still not settled." "They need us to be close by," says Betty. "And besides, Karen, our youngest, says it would just kill her if we sold the house."

Harold and Betty have watched their friends move on. Some have left the state or retired. The two have less interest in the things they have done for thirty years, for very good reason: They are bored. They bicker more, they entertain less, and Betty has resigned from most of the community organizations she used to enjoy. She unconsciously expects more from her daughters than she ever has. This has strained the relationships in ways they had not anticipated. The daughters are puzzled that their formerly easygoing mom is so frequently irritable, and Betty doesn't seem to realize how resentful she has become.

Debbie, Harold, and Betty, all still only in their late fifties, feel they have few choices left. They are stuck in the hourglass with decisions they made decades earlier.

They are unable to see that their insistence that they "have no choice" is itself a choice with many ramifications. The reason for their "stuckness" is not completely apparent: Are they simply putting their children's needs before their own, or do they need to protect themselves from the possibilities that change might present?

> **Paula:** *Empty nest* has such negative connotations, but in reality, it's an opportunity to rede-

ploy resources—and a time to rearrange the relationships in your life. Empty-nest syndrome has
had bad press, because we have not been programmed to think of it as another beginning. We
are programmed to think of it as the end of the
most rewarding arrangement of our lives.

Jeff: But what if parenting wasn't the most satisfying? Or what if, when the kids leave, you actually feel emotionally and financially unburdened?
This should logically be true, but culturally, we
aren't oriented to look at this stage as a beginning
or as a new opportunity. No doubt this negative
viewpoint is a holdover from the child-centered
environment we were raised in, but is not particularly relevant to the self-actualized, focused parents now experiencing empty nest.

Nell and Ned report that the empty-nest syndrome is
highly underrated. "Of course we miss seeing them every day,"
Ned told us. "But it is great to be able to focus more on ourselves. Some of the changes are small—we don't have to keep
the house stocked with the mountains of food required for
growing kids. But some are very big—because we can use our
money in totally different ways. Most people expect you to talk
about how much you miss the kids. And slip into a mild depression for a few months as proof that you really love them. I
love them a lot—even more at a distance!"

Ned and Nell "celebrated" having both kids away at college
by spending a year in London. Ned had been working in Europe for years and commuted home for weekends. Once the
kids were both in school, Nell decided to take a hiatus from her

demanding career. She moved to London to join Ned. Both remember that year as one of their happiest.

"We rented a charming house in Knightsbridge. We felt like newlyweds—except this time, we had money. We knew we were close enough to be home in six hours if there was an emergency. But the distance also provided an enormous relief from all the day-to-day responsibilities that we had taken on over the years." In a bit of a role reversal, they entrusted the supervision of the New York home to their college-aged daughter. "It was good for her," Ned said, "to have the responsibility to check on things. And to know we trusted her to handle it."

Nell and Ned learned a lot from their year abroad. "We hadn't realized how many people are in our lives on a regular basis—friends, family, work associates, people in the community. We love them all—and guess what? They were all there when we returned, but it was very cocoon-like to spend so much time—just the two of us."

Many boomers seem very willing to transfer funds and focus from raising kids to indulging themselves. The pushback may come from the kids themselves, but part of growing up for them is to understand they need us less. The parenting role for those with adult children may be to retool and relax their sense of responsibility—so that a new relationship with kids can emerge. Ideally, that relationship can be one that is less about dependence and more about new experiences.

The kids may need more help with this than the parents do. It is challenging and important to teach our kids again. This time, it is important to teach them not to fear change—that their past and their security is safe within them now, and it doesn't require that their childhood home be maintained as a permanent mausoleum for their memories. It may, in fact, be inspiring for them to see their parents' metamorphosis. It may teach them better than words ever could about the importance of taking control of their lives.

Kids can be an excuse not to change—and an element in getting stuck in the neck of the hourglass. It is understandable that after almost two decades of child-oriented decisions, taking your kids into account in everything you do would be second nature. But they need not be more than that—a consideration. You've paid your dues, done your time. You won't stop loving them or wanting to be with them, but maybe the terms of that can change.

In fact, it is vital that these terms do change. Everyone is an adult now. And although the ties that bind are strong, the best reason to want to see each other is excitement and anticipation—not obligation.

Megan, who is the parent of two kids now in their twenties, feels particularly depressed as she looks ahead to her sixtieth birthday: "I guess we are going to want to live near the kids—and grandkids—but live where? The kids are ten years from settling down."

> **Paula:** This is a typical boomer dilemma. Somewhere embedded in our reptilian brain is a sepia-tinted fantasy of family dinners with three generations present—grandma and grandpa presiding over groaning dining room tables and smiling babies in high chairs.
>
> **Jeff:** We married later, divorced more, had fewer children. Many of us had our kids when we were much older than previous generations. The "old" fantasy won't work for us, if for no other

reason than a difference in chronology. Boomers who delayed childbearing until their midthirties or later, may be seventy by the time grandkids arrive.

Paula: But the more important flaw in the old fantasy is the new set of rules we have played by our entire adult lives. The habit of pursuing self-actualization doesn't abort at fifty or sixty. To maintain our sense of self and well-being, we need to continue to cultivate the people and activities that will fuel us. We need to continue making choices—for ourselves. This is no time to forget that the best and most satisfying elements of our lives have been the result of creative choices.

Jeff: No doubt some of us will enjoy being the center of a multigenerational family—all healthy and eager to spend time together—but most of us will have to be more creative.

Paula: Waiting for the kids to visit—or for the grandkids to arrive—is a game you may or may not win. Not that the kids won't visit; they will. And maybe there will be grandchildren as well. But these expectations are not the linchpins to an exciting and fulfilling middle age—because they are not our choices to make. And they are not in our control.

The Hourglass Effect is a generational epidemic. Even for baby boomers, isolation is one of our concerns and it is strangely helpful to find that we are not in this alone. We are pack animals. Although many of us enjoy days on end of our own company, we still need the companionship of others—if not for the joy of it, then to benchmark our own vital signs. We are all struggling with many of the same issues.

The people you know, and those you used to know, are some of your most important resources in getting in touch with the parts of yourself you want to bring into your future. Greater Adulthood may begin with creating a new map of your people universe. It will force a reconsideration of your past, your own priorities, and your hopes for the future. Who do you want to be with you on this journey, and what role do you want to play? An Hourglass Solution provides the opportunity to develop new relationships and renovate old ones. The people in our lives are critical to the youthful vitality and hopefulness we are seeking in this next stage of life.

5

Getting Energy Back:
Reengaging with the World

Vitality is the elixir that defines youth, and it is a necessary condition for positive change: Energy enables choice. The sorry alternative is passive aging.

Passive aging is the acceptance of a steady decline in health and physical appearance after fifty. Those who have succumbed are softer, slower, less vigorous, and less healthy every time you see them. These symptoms of being stuck in the neck of the hourglass need to be attacked with urgency. Listen to what passive aging sounds like:

> "I'm too tired to do something new. Hell, I'm too tired to go to the movies."

> "I raised a family and built a career. I deserve to relax."

> "I'm relieved, in a way, that I don't want to do new things—new is so much work."

> "I just don't think I have the energy to have fun anymore. Peace and quiet sounds good."

This is the language of stuck, and it is a self-fulfilling prophecy: The more dissatisfied you are with the life you are leading, the less energy you will have to change it. It is insidious and self-defeating, but it need not be a terminal condition.

There are three aspects of personal energy: physical, intellectual, and emotional. Improving your health and personal appearance, awakening your intellectual curiosity, and finding excitement and support from other people are all energy accelerators. They tend to be linked, and their impact is exponential. This chapter is about why your Hourglass Solution needs to address all three.

Feeling Good and Looking Good

Without proactive intervention, physical aging is about gradual diminishment. The decision to fight it every step of the way may be the biggest physical challenge you have ever taken on. It requires diligence, intelligence, and courage, but the reward is that you have created more choices for the future. The longer you stay in shape, stay healthy, and pay attention to your appearance, the more options for the future you will have.

Research over the past forty years has shown a remarkable bias toward personal attractiveness. Physically attractive people are more likely to get hired for a job, are rated as more intelligent, and thought to be overall better people.[1] There is a deep-seated belief that personal appearance is related to competence, social skills, personal confidence, and moral virtue. Juries are even more likely to acquit a physically attractive person. None of this bias is likely to end when a person hits fifty.

Charla Krupp, former beauty director at *Glamour* magazine and author of the best-selling book *How Not to Look Old*, puts it bluntly, "Let's not fool ourselves: looking good is key to keeping our jobs. Many of us have had the experience of being at work and realizing that we are the oldest person around the conference table—and not by a few years. We've reached the age where some of our colleagues are young enough to be our kids. We have to look younger to help level the playing field."[2]

As physical changes sneak up, we acclimate ourselves to them. Less activity today means even less of it a few years from now. Indifference paves the road to incapacity: imperceptible at first, but it is an ever-deepening, downward spiral. Illness and the physical signs of aging may be a statistical inevitability, but leading-edge boomers are refusing to leave their sex lives or physical attractiveness behind them. Aging gracefully means a conscientious plan for damage control. Both men and women diet. They exercise with a competitive zeal they may not have had at twenty. They dye their hair and investigate all means of "wrinkle correction." Moisturizers exist for every body part, and there are hormone replacements for everyone who is suffering the lack of them. Cosmetic dentists have proliferated as fast as cosmetic dermatologists. Some people hire trainers; some go to the gym religiously. Others have surgery, and some just add a little extra walking. We applaud them all. We are enthusiastic about any actions that boomers decide to take to help them ameliorate the age symptoms that interfere with their ability to make choices.

Confronting Reality

Some people assume that their health and physical appearance will decline after 50 and that there is nothing to be done about it. This is simply not true. Dr. Vonda Wright, an orthopedic surgeon at the University of Pittsburgh Medical Center, found that even though almost everyone does slow down as he or she ages, it is possible, through a consistent exercise program, to decelerate the deterioration significantly.[3] It has been assumed that our bodies simply break down as we age, but research has indicated that the process can be slowed considerably. Precise predictions are impossible, but many gerontologists believe that the average person can easily live to be 110 or 115.[4] Exercise at age 40 or 50 or even 60 conclusively produces results.

There are limitations to what can be manipulated, but our physical appearance, in many ways, is as malleable as it has been at all other life stages. We have always made choices about the way we look and altered it to a standard we found acceptable or even pleasing. Finding the balance, however, between overdoing and not doing enough has proved to be difficult for many.

> **Paula:** I'm still struggling with finding that. Balance has never been my strong suit in anything I've ever done, and fitness is no exception. I tend to overdo the exercise thing. When I turned fifty, I studied karate, which might have been a good idea except that I was competing—or I tried to— with men and women half my age. I took two classes a day in a desperate attempt to keep up.
>
> **Jeff:** I've done the same thing myself, but the trouble with that, aside from the risk of hurting yourself, is the ones who push themselves beyond reasonable limits hit the wall and generally shift into neutral for a long time. That's what you want to avoid.

Paula: I think the key is setting reasonable goals, but defining *reasonable* is a complicated issue for me—tempering aspiration and self-acceptance, competitiveness and delusion.

Those who are more relaxed about physical changes may also have a hard time recalibrating as they get older. Too much self-acceptance is as dangerous as having unrealistic standards. Some habits may look benign at first: Move a button on the waistband of your skirt, and then just buy a bigger size.

The title of Peter Keating's article in *SmartMoney Magazine* says it all: "Why Do the Elderly Dress So Badly? No, Really." Keating calls it the "Constanza Line," referring to Jerry Seinfeld's admonishment of George Constanza (from the TV sitcom *Seinfeld)* for wearing sweatpants. "You know the message you're sending out to the world with these? You're telling the world: I give up! I can't compete in normal society. I'm miserable, so I might as well be comfortable."[5] It's clear that too many boomers are crossing the "Constanza Line."

Gaining weight, losing muscle tone, or just caring less and less about your appearance are all symptomatic of getting stuck. Unattended tooth loss and hearing loss are more obvious signals of a loss of self-esteem. It may begin with denial: "I'm not hard of hearing; she's just hard to hear." Theater and movies lose their appeal when the audience is appreciating a line you couldn't hear. Restaurants as a social venue are no longer viable if the background noise obscures the conversation of your companion. The impact is cumulative and geometric in effect.

The trickle-down effect of any concession needs to be acknowledged. The decision to give up one's fitness isn't just one decision—it becomes a series of relinquishments. We accept that it is harder to stay fit and that the results can't be as dramatic. We need to go to more doctors, and it gets more frightening. But hardly anything is as important for success in Greater Adulthood.

Reversing the Tide

When Marilyn had her fiftieth birthday in sight, her sister made her take a hard look at herself. She had put on thirty pounds since her twenties—a few with each child, a few more with every disappointment. That only averages to a pound a year when you think about it. Her dad died the same year she divorced John, her husband of many years. She told us that the weight of those losses "settled around my middle, and since none of my clothes fit very well anymore, I figured the heck with it. I stopped caring about how I looked. In fact, I stopped looking at all. No one else was—why should I?

"But then my older sister came for a visit. She's the kind who just says everything she wants to say. And when I picked her up at the train, she didn't even say hi. She said, 'What the hell happened to you? You look just terrible!' And she kept it up for a whole week. I told her to stop, that it wasn't funny, that I didn't care, that I thought I looked just fine. But by the time she went home, she had me enrolled in Weight Watchers."

Marilyn went on to tell us that Weight Watchers was just the beginning. "Of course, I didn't just look better; I had more energy than I knew what to do with! When I stopped looking like a beached whale, I stopped acting like one. One day, I took my bike out of the garage, pumped up the tires, and—I'm telling you—I felt like a kid. I'm never giving that up again."

Jeff: Marilyn's story was one of many we heard about the impact of getting fit. There are lots of different tactics, but the stories all had one thing in common. The decision to improve physical appearance resulted in a tremendous increase in energy—which, in turn, made other choices viable.

Paula: Unfortunately, we also saw people go the other way. Lots of women told us their bathing-suit days were over. It's a pity, because that meant swimming and boating and beaches were over as well.

Jeff: This was true for men, too. When they gave up their diet and exercise routines, they no longer had the energy for activities like biking or tennis—activities that they had enjoyed for decades. Those losses almost always were followed by withdrawals of other kinds.

The physical health risks associated with being overweight are well known, but there are serious mental risks as well. In a study by Kaiser Permanente among 6,583 men and women aged forty to forty-five, people thirty pounds overweight were 3.6 times as likely to develop dementia.[6] Just in case we needed it, this finding presents another good reason to stay—or get back—in shape.

Medical Intervention

The massive progress against childhood diseases such as polio, German measles, and chicken pox may have convinced boomers that they were invincible. They presumed that the diseases that killed their parents and grandparents were surely not going to kill them. This does not appear to be true without proactive measures.

The typical maladies of aging, from bone loss to hearing impairment, are affecting boomers just as they afflicted their parents. But most boomers are not nearly as stoic about the symptoms. Published by the National Bureau of Economic Research, the University of Pennsylvania and Carleton University conducted a study of boomers' health.[7] The study found that boomers in their fifties today complain of more health problems than the World War II generation did when its members were in their fifties. Boomers experience more pain; a greater number of chronic health problems; and more difficulty walking, climbing stairs, and getting up from a chair.[8]

Some theorists claim that baby boomers are now paying for the excesses of their behavior in the 1960s and 1970s, but just as likely is the notion that they have higher expectations of how they *should* feel as they age. As discussed in Chapter 2, boomers will not easily accept even minor health problems and are likely to seek medical antidotes to whatever ails them, both large and small.

What are realistic expectations for us, as we get older? It remains an open issue, but boomers have a great many medical options to sample, from over-the-counter creams and gels to prescription remedies targeted at aging bodies.

The health and beauty industry spent six billion dollars in advertising in 2006, telling us that we could look and feel younger and convinced us to purchase sixty billion dollars' worth of their products.[9] Whoever said, "It's not nice to fool Mother Nature" was probably not a boomer. Americans, mostly boomers, spent twelve billion dollars on medical cosmetic treatments—

over four million Botox treatments alone.[10] Millions more Americans routinely are injected with synthetic fillers designed for "wrinkle correction." The treatments provide virtually instant relief from disappearing lips and permanent frown lines and laugh lines that have matured into crevasses. Although these treatments will lighten your wallet by thousands of dollars, they offer non-surgical instant gratification.

Plastic surgery used to be available only to the very rich. The democratization of this field is now clear: Boomers of all income brackets can indulge. Charlotte, a hair stylist who earns only slightly above the national average, told us, "People see my hands all day long. I would wear gloves to cover the age spots, but you can't cut hair with gloves on. So I started my own 'Christmas Club' account. Only it wasn't for Christmas presents. When I've saved enough, I'm having laser treatment on my hands." By her last tally, Charlotte was almost there.

Boomers are the lucky beneficiaries of an immense pharmaceutical output intended to provide symptomatic relief for our descent into decrepitude. A sense of humor is essential. While not exactly funny, these non-life-threatening ailments can be fertile ground for humor. The conditions are ubiquitous, and the boomer appetite for prescription drugs has exceeded the most avaricious predictions. Not only are we not in this alone, entire industries have devoted themselves to creating a soft landing for us. For the first time ever, more than half of all insured Americans, led by boomers, are taking prescription medicines regularly for chronic health problems.[11]

We can at midlife, through deliberate intervention, change some physical aspects of our appearance that have bothered us. And we can sometimes correct problems we thought we would have to live with forever.

New techniques have provided many boomers with relief from physical conditions that previously had limited choices. At age fifty-eight, Michael got braces on his teeth to correct a condition that had made him self-conscious his whole life— and had begun to cause medical problems. Bobbie had been a runner for most of her adult life, but gave it up in her fifties because of stress incontinence. "I loved running. It was the only way I had ever kept my weight down, but my incontinence just made it too uncomfortable. It was a big give-up. But last year, a new surgical procedure became available, and it worked! I truly feel young again. It was a miracle!"

The same can be said for hip and knee replacements. Damaged joints used to mean seriously impaired mobility and the end of sports, but boomers are taking advantage of new medical technology for extending their ability to enjoy the physical pursuits of youth. Joint replacements of all kinds are becoming common surgical procedures. In 2001, about 165,000 hips were replaced and 326,000 knees. [12] It was predicted that by 2030, this number will skyrocket to 527,000 and 3.48 million, respectively. [13] Some orthopedic surgeons have even called it an epidemic.

> **Paula:** There is no fountain of youth. Attempts to never grow older are proven nonstarters. We can't turn back the clock, but there are choices to be made.
>
> **Jeff:** There is no need to enumerate the impact of gravity and general wear and tear on the human body. Look in the mirror. Amelioration is possible—not complete reversal or correction. The final adjustment that needs to be made is the way

we think about youth and a cultural standard that equates youth with beauty.

Paula: Acceptance of change is critical. Physical changes are inevitable, but we can choose how we feel about these changes, and we have options for managing them.

Jeff: Making choices is an assertion of control, which certainly feels better than passive aging.

Boomers are too large a group to have a single view on a subject as amorphous as the physical aspects of growing older. There are, however, some recognizable types and much that can be learned. Some people have been very aggressive in the battle against the symptoms of aging. Often these same people were more focused on their appearance in their younger days— but not always. Some took their health and their looks for granted. They thought of it as a natural resource until it began to deplete and only then took corrective action.

At age fifty, we can find joy in physical endeavors that we may have taken for granted at an earlier age. We are also less judgmental of others and ourselves. Norm told us about his weekly basketball games. "I've been playing with some of the same people for thirty years. Thousands of games, I would guess. We shout at each other, whine, compliment good plays, and bemoan our lost skills. The age range in the game is about thirty to sixty. I still think of myself as able to do all sorts of things that I really can no longer do. Every time I try to touch the rim and fail, I'm surprised. Anyway, basketball is a way for me to feel young when I play well, but because the effects of aging are so undeniable, it is also a way to experience and come to terms with aging."

Only you know what is realistic for you. If you were never a great athlete, you probably won't be taking the gold at the Senior Olympics, either. However, there are legions of boomers who started running at forty or fifty and manage a marathon every year. One need not become a marathoner to feel a sense of accomplishment and pride in one's physical ability. Swimming, biking, yoga, Pilates, and walking are all great choices for beginning a fitness program. If you had a routine when you were younger, you already know the ropes. Be reasonable in your goals, and your body will thank you for it.

Erica is an unusually beautiful woman at sixty-one: "Every year, you have to eat less and exercise more. It's not that I diet or starve myself, but every little bit helps. It's just simple math. If you're using fewer calories, you have to take in fewer just to stay even," she said, flashing her movie-star smile. "Last year, I stopped eating bread that wasn't brown.

"Exercise?" she continued, "I was a runner until just last year. Now I do what I guess *you* might call walking. But *I* still call it running."

Christopher, a fifty-five-year-old magazine editor, said it equally simply: "Eat less, and walk every chance you get. You don't need to be a doctor to figure that one out. If you are fatter than you want to be, quit complaining and get moving."

"I had an epiphany in yoga class," Laura told us. "I've gone to yoga off and on for years. There is this thing in yoga class called 'inversions'—head stands, shoulder stands, being upside down. It's supposed to help your circulation and clear blockages in your digestive track. I was in class one day doing a shoulder stand, and I opened my eyes—I usually keep them closed. And I realized that the world looks different when you're upside down. Did that just sound really stupid? Anyway, for me, it made me realize that I've been looking at the world from one perspective my entire life and, frankly, I was getting a little bored. Yoga taught me to see the world from a different perspective."

Although there is a group for whom the pursuit of a fountain of youth has become its own kind of trap, we are agnostic on the question of how much focus is too much. Boomers who are proactive in maintaining their looks and their health are happier and more optimistic. Generally, if the barometer is energy level—and expectations are realistic—those who are actively involved in protecting their physical health and caring for their appearance can then be more aggressive and adventurous in cultivating new options and new relationships.

Prevention and Early Detection

If there was one universal lesson we learned from the boomers we spoke with, it was this: Prevention and early detection through regular checkups has to be a part of your regular body maintenance program in midlife. We believe there is no responsible way around it.

> **Paula:** You really do need to have all the tests your doctor recommends—colonoscopy, mammogram, whatever. No one likes to do it. Everyone is a little apprehensive. But you have to do it.
>
> **Jeff:** In this case, the consequences of inattention are potentially life-threatening. Although many of us have skated through our young adulthood without the benefit of medical attention, it is unlikely that our luck will hold out indefinitely.

Paula: Boomers may live longer than any previous generation—but only because modern medicine can identify lethal conditions and treat them successfully. If you are not proactive about your own health, then you cannot expect to claim the rewards that our generation is heir to.

Jeff: There are always a million reasons not to take care of your health—but they are all symptomatic of stuck. You are not brave—you are stuck— if you resist or reject the available wisdom of preventative medicine.

Stoic inattention to minor maladies is a matter of choice. Decisions concerning treatment must always be personal. Choosing not to make your own health a priority is a different kind of decision. It is likely to leave you in a position in which you have lost control and consequently have no choices left.

As discussed in Chapter 3, the language we use to talk about ourselves is symptomatic of our approach to aging. The language of stuck is pervasive in the way we talk about fitness and medical care:

"I don't believe in doctors."

"My dad lived until he was ninety-two and never saw a doctor."

"I just don't have time."

"I feel fine, just a little tired. That's to be expected at my age."

"It's impossible to lose weight after menopause."

"What's the point? I'm never going to look like that again."

"I don't go anywhere. Why do I need new clothes?"

Jeff: We heard each of the preceding statements many times, and we became acutely attuned to what the hidden message in this kind of language really is. Each message sends up a red flag that the person had lost sight of the many options open and was unnecessarily accepting limitations.

Paula: We may be unable to avoid getting stuck in the hourglass. It seems to happen to almost everyone, but staying stuck is a choice.

Jeff: That doesn't mean that you are in control of everything that happens. We will all get sick and we will all die of something, but now more than ever, we need to find a place between fear and fatalism.

Paula: Few of us could look like a fashion model in our twenties, and we can't look thirty-five now. But that doesn't mean we throw in the towel. This is no time to stop trying. In fact, it is the perfect time to try a little harder.

Boomers are by nature and experience a proactive lot. The Hourglass Solution is a personal solution. The only universal requirement is that you focus on what you really want and insure that you have the energy to create possibilities and make choices. We are lucky to have so many options available for helping us preserve our vitality. As a generation, we have a wealth of experience in manipulating our bodies. Whatever your preference—diet, exercise, drugs, surgery, or constant vigilance—the importance of sustaining a physical energy level that is enabling cannot be overestimated.

Intellectual Energy

Intellectual energy is a singularly important part of the Hourglass Solution. Just as with physical energy and appearance, it requires some effort to stay in good mental form. Again, society seems to give strong cultural messages that undermine our determination to stay mentally fit. Fortunately, reality is on our side.

Research on brain chemistry has shown that new experiences activate the brain with dopamine and norepinephrine.[14] This is the same chemical reaction that is ignited during the early stages of romantic love. This is a good thing. It means that the excitement and anticipation of love is accessible to all of us on many levels.

"I remember my Aunt Katie telling me when I was a teenager that she tried to learn something new every year. She was in her forties at the time, and I must have been really impressed because I never forgot it and have really tried to do it, even if it's just a little thing." Tina, a receptionist at a dentist's office in Tampa, told us this story and then went on to recount the new things she had learned in the last few years. "One year, I started Pilates; then I learned to knit. I got back on roller skates after thirty years—I counted that as new. I learned to play chess, and now I'm studying American antique furniture. I'd like to learn to grow orchids." Then she chuckled, "My husband keeps suggesting that I learn to cook."

"It doesn't matter what your next new thing is," Steve, said, "as long as you keep adding, not subtracting." Steve is an intellectual, a self-professed "idea man." He told us with notable irony about his latest passion. "Norma is my love, and she has made me feel better and more alive than I have in years." Norma is a brindled pit-bull mix that Steve adopted when his career became less demanding. "She was a rescue, a real handful, but she changed my life. First, because she got me outside several times a day. But as I got to know her, I was fascinated by her athleticism. I'm not an athlete myself, but watching her was a real out-of-body experience. The most compelling part was training her. It wasn't easy, because I had to learn a whole new way of communicating and a new vocabulary that had nothing to do with words."

Both Tina and Steve have experienced the exhilaration of learning new things and will personally attest to the feeling of well-being they associate with cultivating new interests. Scientists, especially neuroscientists, confirm that the active, exercised brain is a happy brain. Neuroplasticity, a subject currently creating great excitement among medical researchers, describes physical changes that take place in the brain as a result of new experiences and new information. In other words, our brains are reconfigured as a result of the thoughts we have—even as adults.

Gene Cohen, director of the Center for Aging, Health and Humanities at George Washington University, explained it in lay terms: "Dozens of new findings are overturning the notion that 'you can't teach old dogs new tricks.' We've learned that older brains can process information in a dramatically different way than younger brains. Older people can use both sides of their brains for tasks that younger people use only one side to accomplish. A great deal of scientific work has also confirmed the 'use it or lose it' adage: the mind grows stronger from use and from being challenged in the same way that muscles grow stronger from exercise. The brain can grow entirely new brain cells—a stunning finding filled with potential"[15]

Aside from the obvious implications for degenerative diseases such as Alzheimer's and the rehabilitative possibilities for stroke victims, the everyday news is that our brains seem to retain their plasticity even in later life and that plasticity can be measurably improved by continuous learning. The good news is we can improve the functioning of our brains—even very late in life.

This also suggests that although it may not be easy to reprogram personality characteristics or personal habits, it is possible to do so at any age. Our brains are not hardwired: We can "rewire" at any time.

The scientific data confirms what we know intuitively. One of the most debilitating symptoms of passive aging is boredom. It is also a symptom of stuck. Listen to the language of intellectual stuck:

> "I'm too old to learn anything new."

> "My concentration is gone. I can't even read a book."

> "It seems like I've forgotten half of what I used to know."

Even phrases like *senior moment* reveal a passive acceptance of a quality of aging that inhibits choice. Only 1 percent of adults aged fifty to sixty-five actually have Alzheimer's, and only 5 percent of those aged sixty-five to seventy-four.[16] Alzheimer's disease and other forms of dementia are *not* a normal part of aging, and yet complaints about memory loss are ubiquitous in this age group. We think this is another aspect of stuck. A so-called senior moment is seldom a precursor to senility. It is more often caused by a lack of sleep, stress, or undue distractions and is sometimes simply an excuse for being mentally lazy.

> **Jeff:** I read recently that the reason we have trouble retrieving names and information isn't about forgetting—it is about the vast amount of information we have stored by the time we reach our age. A toddler knows only a dozen people and so can easily sort through the names and faces.
>
> **Paula:** So, that's the cocktail-party problem. "I know I know that person—but from where?"
>
> **Jeff:** Exactly. You are literally sorting through the thousands of people you know and trying to match not just face and name, but time and place as well.
>
> **Paula:** And, of course, toddlers don't get embarrassed when they don't remember a name—the older person certainly does. And the more anxious you become, the bigger the mental block.

New interests beget new interests and energy. In spite of a youth-obsessed culture that seems to shout that younger brains are better, research suggests that this is simply not the case. Although it may take you longer to learn new information, once you have it, the new knowledge stays with you as well as it does with younger people. And there is evidence that older people are often better at complex analytical thinking. They are more flexible in their problem-solving strategies and have cooler heads in a crisis. Sara Reistad-Long, a reporter for the *New York Times*, recently spoke with Lynn Hasher, a professor of psychology at the University of Toronto and a senior scientist at the Rotman Research Institute, about her research on the comparative brain and memory functions of older individuals. Her conclusion is that the older brain may indeed be the wiser one. "A broad attention span may enable older adults to ultimately know more about a situation and the indirect message of what's going on than their younger peers. We believe that this characteristic may play a significant role in why we think of older people as wiser."[17]

Why, then, do so many of us complain of memory loss and deterioration in mental quickness? We are very suggestible. Yale social psychologist Becca Levy found that people who were shown negative words like *senile* before taking memory tests did worse than those who were given a positive suggestion.[18] In other words, if you buy into the idea that you are losing your edge, you probably will. Agility is mental as well as physical, and body maintenance needs to extend from head to toe.

In Hillsdale, New York, a new kind of intellectual community meets every Saturday at noon to discuss issues that range from the economy to the arts to religion. They call themselves the OBs—the Old Boys. They range in age from early forties to late eighties, and the discussion is always lively. Many of the members are tremendously successful in their fields, which range from economics to psychiatry, history, and law. Many are published authors. Some are retired, and others continue to work. Each session begins with a presentation by a member who has spent considerable time researching his subject. For some, this requires learning new things, but, at minimum, requires that they bring themselves up-to-date on topics that they used to know well.

The group has grown from a nucleus of about eight to almost thirty regulars. The highly entertaining and literate summaries of their meetings go out to an e-mail list of sixty people, which include wives, daughters, and other interested parties who live too far away to get to the meetings. These men are committed to staying current and intellectually active and have found an interesting and cooperative social forum for doing so.

> **Paula:** My dad is an Old Boy, and I'm on their mailing list. I have suggested to them that the summaries of their meetings are, in my opinion, book worthy. I think they are that good.
>
> **Jeff:** Although the Old Boys are uniquely credentialed, affinity groups like this are sprouting up all over the country—grassroots social networking based on some shared interest—from politics to pasta making.
>
> **Paula:** The Old Boys, and groups like them, are doing on an informal basis what many colleges and universities are doing more formally.
>
> **Jeff:** When I was in college in the 1970s, the school let anyone who lived in Williamstown audit courses for free. At most, there were a handful of people who took advantage of this. Today, there are more people over sixty asking to sit in on classes than there is room.

Other than English-as-a-second-language programs, the fastest-growing segment of education today is aimed at the continuing education of older Americans.[19] Almost every major university in the country is expanding its programs, which already range from art appreciation to medieval philosophy, and is anticipating significant increases in enrollment as boomers' leisure time and desire to flex their intellectual muscle increase. Because of their low cost and easy accessibility, community colleges are at the forefront of this effort. Already, 6 percent of community college students are over fifty. That percentage will surely increase in the next few years.[20]

According to Alvaro Fernandez, the founder of Sharp-Brains (a company dedicated to "using emerging technologies to keeping our brains healthy and productive as long as possible"), the brain fitness industry is young but growing at 50 percent a year. He estimates that it will become a two-billion-dollar business by 2015.[21]

The hurdle will be to overcome the sense of inertia and low expectations that are symptomatic of being stuck in the hourglass. Boomers who expect adventure must not let their intellectual energy or confidence erode. Use it or lose it. Science has confirmed that.

Emotional Energy

Loss of emotional energy—the twinkle in your eye and the curiosity about other people—is by far the most insidious symptom of passive aging. It is a psychological issue of great magnitude. There are many causes: loss, isolation, inactivity, boredom, and stress. Sometimes it is situational, and sometimes it is chronic.

Unlike physical or intellectual energy, there is no clear measure of emotional energy. Psychologists have typically called it *subjective well-being* and use a combination of measures, including self-esteem, optimism, depression, social support, and locus of control, as surrogates for an overall index.[22]

One of the most interesting measures of emotional well-being is the Gallup-Healthways Well-Being Index.[23] For many years, Gallup has been tracking how Americans feel and has surveyed over 100,000 Americans in 2008 alone. With this extensive experience and base of data, Gallup has determined seven items that, together, can measure an individual's emotional state of well-being on a daily basis. Just thinking about yesterday, ask yourself these questions:

- Were you treated with respect?

- Did you have enough energy to get things done?

- Did you smile or laugh a lot?

- Did you learn or do something interesting?

- Did you feel well rested?

- Did you eat healthy all day?

- Did you worry about money?

Jeff: All these issues are associated with aging in this culture—and most of them are under your control.

Paula: We've specifically talked about quite a few and will cover more in the rest of this chapter and the next two. Each question provides the opportunity for choice making.

> **Jeff:** I admit, I did post this list on my bath-room mirror for a few weeks.
>
> **Paula:** Why? To block the view?

Effective treatment for a lack of emotional energy begins with recognizing the symptoms. Some people who are stuck in the neck of the hourglass find it very difficult to acknowledge their own pain. They have been playing by other people's rules for so long they lose track of what their own choices could be. Duties and responsibilities are central to adult life, but when they drown out our own voices and close off options, it can make us sick and tired.

Overcommitment

The phenomenon of the sandwich generation is well documented: Boomers are caught between the needs of their children and those of their parents. According to a Pew Research Center report, nearly ten million boomers are currently providing assistance to both their adult children and their parents.[24] Some in the sandwich generation actually experience the "club sandwich with all the trimmings"—adult children and grandchildren who need help, as well as aging parents who need more assistance—all while they are still working themselves. The stress of overcommitment is a sure way to lose track of what you want. One can sustain saying yes to everyone, and by default no to yourself, for only so long. Emotional energy is like a bank account: Making too many withdrawals with no deposits leaves one emotionally drained.

It is important to distinguish between an emergency, a set of events that require immediate attention, and an ongoing state of affairs that will rob you irrevocably of your emotional energy. Only you can decide what is too much, but learning to say no, even to a small request, can be very empowering. The ability to take care of *you* is a prerequisite for taking care of others. One boomer told us a hard-learned lesson about protecting herself.

"I am a good caregiver," Laura told us. "I've done it my whole life, and it's something that I am proud of. I raised a couple of difficult kids, nursed a sick husband, and cared for my mother until her death. It was natural for me to offer to help my friend Denise after she was divorced. She was quite down on her luck and in serious debt. I offered to let her stay with me until she could get back on her feet. At the time, I didn't realize that she was the give-an-inch-take-a-mile type.

"My 'what am I doing to myself?' moment occurred nine months into this arrangement, when I realized I had stopped seeing other friends because Denise's neediness was wearing me out. She was sucking me dry. She paid for nothing and gave nothing. I'm a good person, not a doormat. I asked her to leave the next day. And then I had a party."

Our friend's instinct to rekindle her emotional energy by having a party was a good one. Social engagements can give us an infusion of new energy and new people. Have a party, and ask each of your guests to bring someone you don't already know. You'll be surprised at who shows up. And how many new friends you might make.

"Claire and I love to entertain," Artie explained. "But after living in the same town for nearly fifty years, we were surprised to realize that we were just entertaining each other. The same group of people showed up at every party we went to. Last year, Claire and I were invited to a party and were told that we couldn't come unless we brought a new person—someone who nobody else knew. It sounded like a terrible idea—so hokey. But it turned out to be the best party of the year. We've done it ourselves—twice."

Jeff: This is a very good time to attend a high school or college reunion. Personally, I'm surprised at how close I've become to some of my fellow alumni—even ones I didn't really know in college. We share a common four years, and that can ground a relationship.

Paula: It's also a good time for a reunion of former colleagues.

Jeff: I'm a big fan of that, as well. One of the ad agencies I used to work for closed down about a dozen years ago. Last year, I decided it was time for a reunion, so I planned one. Over 250 people showed up—and they are begging for another.

Paula: If you hear yourself saying, "I'm not the reunion type," get over it. Are you saying you are better than everyone else who is attending? If that's the case, then attending should be no problem. "I've never been to a reunion"—all the more reason to try it once. "I'm not good at these things"—perhaps you are playing an old tape. Sounds stuck to me.

Jeff: Touching base with others with whom you shared a common experience can be very helpful in sorting out new identities. You will undoubtedly be surprised at something. You may get a different take on how much you have changed or how little. You may rekindle an old friendship. You may get an idea that will be interesting or useful.

Paula: If you don't go, you won't know.

Illness and Personal Loss

It is a near statistical certainty that bad things will happen to you in your life. There will surely be death, disease, sadness, and tragedy. You will certainly face failures and unwanted surprises.

We talked with several boomers who had been derailed by serious illness in midlife. Most survived, and many recovered completely. For some, it was a life-changing experience, while others picked up exactly where they had left off before they became ill. Everyone agreed that dealing with illness required new skills and enormous commitment to getting better.

The first reaction to the occurrence of a serious or potentially life-threatening illness before the age of sixty is, inevitably, shock and disbelief. "How could this be? I am only fifty-four . . . or fifty-seven or fifty-nine. Old people get sick. I'm not old; this can't be true." Denial, as we have seen, is a powerful force in many contexts, but never more potent than when a person is confronting illness. We heard story after story from boomers who ignored significant symptoms until these signs could no longer be ignored.

Serious illness is another country. It is a place that is separate and distinct from good health. Some get there very slowly and some almost instantly, but the universal quality of the experience is accelerated aging. Suddenly, one becomes aware of one's own mortality. Nearly everyone describes debilitating fatigue and the necessity to reevaluate priorities. Recovery often requires finding deep inner resources when one's normal energy source has failed.

Jay had already had a skirmish with death well before he reached the age of fifty. He had suffered a serious case of meningitis while traveling abroad in his late forties. "I was in a coma for ten days," he told us. His recovery was definitely in doubt. But the prayed-for miracle occurred and Jay returned home and continued his life with all the gusto that had always been a distinguishing characteristic.

When he was fifty-four, he started experiencing mild headaches along with occasional nausea and dizziness. As a professional photographer and filmmaker, he attributed his symptoms to a change in eyesight. He was sure that he just needed new glasses and postponed a visit to the eye doctor to "some time down the road when it would be more convenient."

Then he blacked out and crashed his car into a tree. He and his passenger escaped serious injury, but at the hospital where he was taken after the accident, a malignant mass was found under his skull. Jay was suffering from brain cancer. He had surgery and a course of chemotherapy and is now in remission.

"This illness did change my life," he said. "Meningitis was an event that came and went. But this was life changing. I lost a full year of my life. It was a complete year of dealing with nothing else except illness, fatigue, and depression. Now it seems like a year out of context. I am back now, but I was gone. It changed what is important to me. I am clearer than I have ever been about what I do and don't want to do: I want a simpler lifestyle. I want to move to an easily manageable house. I don't want to work so much. I only want to do projects that really excite me. I don't want to waste a moment with people I don't enjoy. So I guess it was good in that way. But I lost a year of my life—an entire year."

Jay fought his way back with a lot of support from his wife of thirty years and many close friends. He marvels at both how ill he once was and his recovery. He says he thinks more about fate and destiny and the power of these forces in our lives. "I am a more spiritual person now; I often think about mortality. Every passing day brings gratitude to the unseen but a deeply felt deity."

Jay entered the "other country" of illness in the split second of his car crash. For Anita, it was a slower trip. It took two years to get to diagnosis and treatment.

Anita had experienced her share of illnesses, but all within the normal and to-be-expected range. She had had five children and was no stranger to the tricks the human body can play on us. "I first noticed that my voice was shaking for no apparent reason. I finally told my husband that something was wrong, and he said that he knew it, too. I went to my primary care doctor, who took a chest x-ray and said that I was very tall and perhaps my breath wasn't able to get all the way up. I went to a pulmonary doctor, who changed my asthma and allergy medicine. My sister-in-law sent me to an ear, nose, and throat (ENT) specialist in the city, and he said to come back for a hearing test. I went to a local ENT, who prescribed heartburn medicine. When that didn't help, he just stopped the medicine.

"I became convinced I had cancer. It was terrible, lonely, and frightening. I began searching the Internet and found that a neurological disorder called spasmodic dysphonia (which is in the Parkinson's disease family) matched my symptoms. I went back to the local ENT, who took a videotape of my vocal cords and he asked me if I had ever heard of spasmodic dysphonia. He was very surprised when I said, 'Yes I have, and I think I have it.'

"The treatment is Botox. I get shots every three to four months. No matter the dosage, it doesn't seem to kick in for about four weeks. I whisper, then squeak and squawk for a month and then have a ninety percent normal voice for about six weeks. Then it starts to deteriorate."

Anita is philosophical: "It could be worse—much worse." But it has clearly changed her life. An animated and talented storyteller, she now measures her words. She has learned to rely on e-mail for communicating with her large family and plans her schedule around the now-familiar cycle of treatments. They are painful and inconvenient and work less and less effectively, but Anita continues to say, "It could be worse," though now with some irony.

> **Paula:** My own experience with illness was a little like Anita's in that it was very difficult to diagnose. I had an autoimmune syndrome that laid me low for several years. The worst of it was severe anemia, which required transfusions every couple of months. Like Anita, there was a cycle. But on the downturn, I had so little energy I could barely function, let alone do the things that were important to me.
>
> **Jeff:** Those were the years where you disappeared from the rest of the world. A lot of people, including me, really lost touch with you.
>
> **Paula:** It takes a great deal of energy to stay in touch, and energy was what I was very short on.

> In the weeks before each transfusion, I could liter-
> ally just do one thing a day. If I met someone for
> lunch, that was about all I could manage.
>
> **Jeff:** Knowing you before and after, I can't
> imagine that.
>
> **Paula:** It was an altered state. And very de-
> pressing. When you are sick for a long time, it is
> almost impossible to imagine being well again.
> And when you are well, you can't really recall
> what it was like to be sick.

Becoming ill is not something we choose; it happens, sometimes even when every precaution has been taken and preventive measures duly practiced. However, illness does present many choices: choice of doctors, treatment, and attitude. The power of optimism is widely acknowledged, but there has been some interesting research on the difference between trying to live and trying not to die. The literature calls it *survivorship*.

"Life-threatening diseases leave little to human jurisdiction," says Corinne Asturias, a consumer strategist for Iconoculture, "but the one thing we can strive to control is attitude. Survivorship gives the struggle a positive focus and punches up a lesson anyone can learn from: Make the most of your days. It's the difference between fulfilled living and a living death."[25] Emotional energy may be your best source of strength when facing the challenge of illness, even when your physical energy is unavailable.

When we first began to interview boomers for this book, we knew that we needed to address this topic, but we weren't prepared for the stories we heard and the insights we gained. People do grow from adversity. Author Po Bronson discovered this while writing *What Should I Do with My Life?* "In hard times people usually changed the course of their lives; in good times, they frequently only talked about change."[26]

Serious illness and loss are the most difficult tragedies for us to endure. We were relieved, consequently, to discover how many people turned these difficult events into a life-affirming experience, and upon further investigation, we discovered that such a positive response to tragedy is not unusual.

George A. Bonanno, a psychology professor at Columbia University and principal investigator on PURL (Project to Understand Reactions to Loss), is one of the foremost experts on the topic of the individual's response to disastrous life events. He found that "a growing body of evidence suggests that most adults exposed to potentially traumatic events are resilient" and that those over sixty-five are especially so.[27] Bonanno categorizes three primary methodologies of resilient behavior: Some turn to family and friends, some turn to books and support groups, and some turn inward to reflect on the pain.

Barb is an example of the third approach. A New England homemaker through and through, she was born and raised in southern Vermont, was married at nineteen, and raised three kids. Her husband, Harvey, had worked for the local electric utility his entire life. By the time she was forty-six, her kids had grown up and moved away. She was forty-nine when Harvey was diagnosed with emphysema.

She nursed him when he was able to be at home, and she sat by his bed every day when he was in the hospital. When Harvey died three years later, she was empty. "Every little piece of me was gone. Pfffft. Just disappeared. I'd given it to the kids and to Harvey. There was nothing left to give anybody."

Barb tried to continue her life almost as if nothing had changed. She called her kids every day and took care of Harvey's three hunting dogs just as if he'd need them again one day. "Harvey just loved those dogs. To me, as long as they were around, he was around. But when one of them died, it really hit me. Harvey was dead, and I finally knew that my life had to change."

Barb started thinking about herself and focusing on her own needs for the first time in over twenty years. She lost weight, dyed her hair, started walking at least a mile every day, and joined a local woman's glee club, even though she hadn't sung since high school.

"I still think about Harvey every day, and I miss him every day. But I'm a much stronger person today than I was then. Two years ago, I was diagnosed with a serious illness. If I had been the old Barb, I'd be dead. But I think I've beaten it, and so does my doctor. When I'm taking my walk in the morning, I talk to Harvey. I know that if he were still here, I'd be dead. When he was alive, there was no 'me' to fight for."

Barb's success in transforming negative life events into positive energy, like Joanna's in the previous chapter, grew from their understanding that they had the right, perhaps the obligation, to focus on themselves. They realized that they had choices, and by defining them, they took control of situations that were potentially very grim.

A "fresh loss" or a catastrophic illness is a three-alarm fire, a calamity that needs attention. Appropriate grief is part of the healing process, but allowing old losses to control the future is crippling. Part of the great news implicit in an Hourglass Solution is that there is a pathway back, even after tragedy.

Paula: This is important—no one can tell you how long to mourn—or how to manage your own illness. But adjusting to a "new normal" is part of finding your energy after a loss, and it requires that you make choices and take control, even after the unimaginable occurs.

Jeff: The death of a loved one is a traumatic event, but the vast majority of people bounce back—only a small subset of people actually suffer from long-term posttraumatic stress disorder.

Paula: Those who continue to suffer are unable to integrate the impact of an experience that was outside their normal frame of reference. Illness and the death of loved ones are universal experiences, and recovery requires that we accept their ubiquity.

Happier people live longer, and a wide range of studies has confirmed this: Hostility, anxiety, and depressive symptoms are risk factors for cardiovascular disease and can actually be considered aging accelerators.[28] Patients who are depressed after a serious illness or operation (such as heart bypass surgery) are more than twice as likely to die within the next five years as are patients who evidence a more positive attitude.[29] Even in dealing with the loss of a loved one or a serious illness, we can make choices, and those choices grant control in an otherwise out-of-control circumstance. Adversity can have benefits, but only if negative life events can be turned into positive emotional energy.

Become Visible Again

Energy attracts attention. And whether it is physical, intellectual, or emotional energy, the less you have, the less attention you get.

When we are young, we take that kind of attention for granted. Sometimes we even find it tiresome. And then one day, you realize it is over. No one is looking. No one is paying attention, but perhaps you aren't, either.

Getting noticed is about staying engaged with the world. It is a two-way street. It is through this engagement that we replenish our energy source. In youth, we engage with others through many levels of flirtation, but getting noticed is not entirely about appearances; it is about engagement. Any kind of engagement, no matter how trivial, is better than the lack of it. Relating to the world takes many forms, and Greater Adulthood means not giving up on any of them without seriously considering the choice that is being made. Greater Adulthood means making positive choices—not acquiescing to negative ones.

You may never stop traffic as you might have in your youth, but if you send out some energy, it is likely you will get some back. The reason we like to be noticed when we are young is it is a way of relating to others, however briefly, and it makes us feel good. As we get older, we need to find other ways to relate and be relevant for all the same reasons.

Jeff: For me, making eye contact with people—whether it's your doorman or a school crossing guard or the woman at the diner who pours your coffee—helps a lot because then they relate to you, even if it's just to return a smile. Make yourself say something to the cashier at the grocery store or the UPS man. Your energy will be rewarded with more. Every encounter can provide some, and the impact is geometric.

Paula: Get a cute dog—that works, too. Invisibility is very real as you get older, but I was really surprised at how much attention came my way when I got a new puppy. Everybody on the street noticed, and all of a sudden, people started smiling at me again. Some even stopped to chat. I'd say it's as good as getting whistled at.

Jeff: Which, of course, you hated—when you were young.

Enormous energy is required to build a new life, and energy may be in short supply for boomers as they face the many issues that have trapped them in the neck of the hourglass. Ironically, loss of energy is a symptom of the problem, but finding it again is an essential element in creating the solution. The causes of loss of vitality are as varied and complex as the life experiences that have brought us to this point, but the antidote is equally personal. Take a walk or a yoga class, join a book club, get a dog—do anything that seems exciting. Everything you actively choose will provide new energy and is part of creating your own Hourglass Solution. Greater Adulthood is powered by your body, brain, and heart: Keep all three fully charged.

6

Our Work:
Risk, Renewal, and Retirement

M any boomers have been defined by their work: It provided an identity and a sense of purpose, as well as the means to create a lifestyle. This was true for homemakers and retailers, brain surgeons and artists, teachers and Wall Street tycoons. Some worked very hard: Boomers made the seventy-hour workweek commonplace in many fields. Others learned to work from home. Some were very ambitious and set new goals as each one was achieved. People moved to different places for their jobs, and for some, global travel become almost routine.

Boomers were the first generation for which two-income families became the norm, with 80 percent of female baby boomers working outside the home. This generation was also the first predominately white-collar generation, comprising more than 60 percent of the workforce.[1] Boomers changed jobs an average of ten times before they were fifty, and 20 percent were laid off at least once.[2] They learned to use a computer and cell phones and BlackBerry smart phones. They looked for fun and personal fulfillment in their work and expected their careers to provide access to their authentic selves. Previous generations found these values in family, religion, and, sometimes, love of country. For boomers, young adulthood was shaped by their work experience, and the transition to Greater Adulthood is likely to be characterized by the relationship to work as well.

Our work lives have been a recipe with many ingredients and variations: The opportunity of midlife is to determine if our needs are still well serviced by our work and if it still provides us with a meaningful identity and a sense of purpose. Financial considerations are always bound up with decisions about work, but we found that people tend to let those requirements drive the entire decision process. That may have made sense in the first half of adult life, but we believe finances ought to be considered independently now. In Chapter 7, the role that money plays in constructing an Hourglass Solution will be discussed separately. But in this chapter, we will simply ask, is your work still working? If it is, then the challenge is to maximize your options for the future. If it's not, your challenge is about creating new choices. Your Hourglass Solution needs to address this important component of your life.

Jeff: Some people are still going strong. They love what they're doing and intend to keep at it for the foreseeable future.

Paula: A good many of us are no longer happy with our work lives, yet face the prospect of retirement with trepidation.

Jeff: The transition from a physical-labor society to a white-collar society has made it difficult for people to know when to stop working, but it could be that stress has replaced physical labor as the most debilitating aspect of a job today.

Paula: We also met dozens of people who are still employed—but are scared that they will be fired at any moment. The social contract between employer and employee that held a place for those with seniority is all but dead. In its wake are fear and uncertainty.

Jeff: The unique challenges of midlife may have made our work life part of the bottleneck, but clear-eyed assessment of your situation can make breaking free a life-changing event.

Paula: There are a million stories, but essentially three categories of outcome: Sticking with the work you have done, using those skills in another way, or retirement, however you may choose to define that. This chapter is a guide to identifying those choices and staying in control of them.

Staying the Course

For some boomers, work was a calling: From a very young age, they knew what they wanted to be, and they then pursued a course of action to get themselves there. Others just happened upon occupations that fulfilled them. Close to half of those aged fifty to fifty-five say they are reasonably satisfied with their jobs, and about one-fifth of boomers are still enthusiastic.[3] Their Hourglass Solution begins with making sure that people can in fact continue their work into the future.

Women who believe they fought a pioneer's battle for equal opportunity in their chosen careers may be particularly reluctant to make a change in their work lives in midlife. They often feel that it took them longer than men to achieve positions of power and are just hitting their full stride. Women who began their careers after raising a family or who took time off to have their children may want to continue working long after their male peers have tired of their work.

Annette is an outgoing and stylish woman in her late fifties. She told us she intends to continue to work at her law firm as long as she possibly can. Her firm has a mandatory retirement age of sixty-seven, but she and several other woman hope to change that. "It took me longer than the men to make partner. Then I took a few years off to have children. Men my age at the firm have already made a great deal of money and are tired of the kind of cases I still find really challenging. I'm still learning and, frankly, having more fun than I ever did. All those years when my kids were small and I was feeling pulled in two directions—that was difficult. This is more like it. I can work late without conflict and enjoy the company of colleagues. I even have time for professional groups now, and I like mentoring younger women—this is really the time of my life."

Entrepreneurs and independent contractors have more apparent control. Doctors and lawyers who have practiced on their own may have the option to continue their work way beyond traditional retirement age and have other choices that could provide maximum flexibility.

Those who work in corporate life, however, face greater career jeopardy as they get older. The solution is less obvious. Iconoculture, a company that analyzes major trends, has called "change and learning the new job security. The desire to control the career path pressures workers to self-manage careers, continuously expanding their skill set and portfolio of assets."[4] It predicts that there will no longer be permanent employees, rather a workforce of nomadic, self-managed "free agents."

Whatever we call it, it will require planning and an acute instinct for self-protection.

> **Paula:** Jeff, you're the last man standing in our business. You must be the oldest living ad man. How do you do it?
>
> **Jeff:** It requires planning and an acute instinct for self-protection.
>
> **Paula:** You know, I do regret leaving before the "gray eminence" stage. I will always wonder if there really are people in their late fifties or early sixties, sitting in corner offices, spouting wisdom to eager young lads and lassies. Is that what you do, Jeff?
>
> **Jeff:** When it doesn't conflict with moat building and naps.

Time for a Change

The reasons for making a change are numerous. Some people no longer find the identity support or sense of purpose they used to from their work. They are merely tired of doing what they have always done. Perhaps their enthusiasm has been diminished by the realization that they are unlikely to find further advancements. Sometimes, the stressful nature of their job has worn them out.

Sometimes, people are simply not as satisfied as they expected to be. Historically, job satisfaction has increased with age, possibly because older workers had better jobs, but this is not necessarily the case for boomers.[5] The Conference Board, a global, nonprofit organization that focuses on management and marketplace issues, recently released a report that found declines in job satisfaction across all ages and income levels and that a quarter of American workers say that they show up for work simply to "collect a paycheck."[6]

Those who do collect a paycheck may consider themselves lucky, because thirty million U.S. workers—most of them boomers—have been "downsized" since the 1980s.[7] Downturns in the economy, corporate cost-cutting, and flatter management structures are just a few of the reasons that no one's job is secure today. It's highly likely that the current recession will hit boomers particularly hard. The truth of the pay system in corporate America is that seniority is expensive, but not necessarily valued.

> **Jeff:** The longer you hang around, the more you get paid—even small raises can add up over the years. As a boss myself, I rationalize annual raises because I think that experience should be rewarded.
>
> **Paula:** But it doesn't necessarily mean that you do the job better than a younger, cheaper person would. Jeff, remember the "purge of the old people" at your former ad agency? That was probably twenty years ago. You and my husband were both working there. Phil came home and an-

nounced "today was the purge of the old people."
A very Phil phrase.

Jeff: Gray hair suddenly became a real liability
in advertising. It didn't matter that you knew all
the ins and outs of your job. They could always
hire a kid who would work twice as hard and get
paid half as much.

Often we don't see it coming. Georgia didn't. "I was vice
chairman and creative director at one of the biggest direct marketing companies in the world. We had had a couple of rounds
of layoffs, and they were extremely painful—because I was the
one who had to make the cuts and tell the people. So one day,
the CFO [chief financial officer] asks me out for a drink. It was
four P.M., so I thought something might be up.

"The first thing he says is, 'There are going to be more layoffs.' I thought, 'God, not again.' And then he said, 'Georgia,
your name is on the list.' I thought, 'That can't be. I'm in the
Direct Marketing Hall of Fame. I'm the most famous person at
the agency. I wrote a bloody best-selling book on direct marketing. They can't fire me.' But they did. It was the biggest
shock of my life. Still is."

Andrew, aged fifty-three and a manager at a plant in upstate New York, told us how he feels about his job: "I remember when I was at the big orientation meeting in college. I went
to the State University of New York at Binghamton. All the
freshmen were seated together, getting prepped for what was
going to happen. The dean stood up and said, 'Shake the hand
of the person on your left. Then shake the hand of the person
on your right. One of the three of you will be gone by the end

of the year.' That's how I feel about work these days. There's an office on my left and an office on my right. Which one of us is going to get laid off this year? It hasn't happened to me yet, but I think it's just a matter of time."

Andrew is almost correct. Eighteen percent of Americans report being laid off in the past three years.[8] What's more, 5 percent of the boomer workforce has completely disappeared.[9] The likelihood of getting fired increases every year. In a world where costs are escalating and technology approximates the value of experience, your job is not an entitlement. The opposite is true: You become more of a balance-sheet liability with every pay raise. And to make matters worse, it takes boomers 50 percent longer to find a new job after being fired than it does younger workers.[10]

Emilie worked in retail from the time she was twenty—and she did very well for twenty-five years. She rose through the ranks and worked at many prestigious companies. But retail—especially fashion retail—is a "young people's business." She lost her job through nonprejudicial circumstances in her mid-forties, and it was very difficult to find a new position. "It really took a lot of work," she told us, "to find that next job. I worked at looking for a job like it was a job for a full year and a half." The job she ended up with paid less than she had made in ten years, but she was happy to have it. Then she got laid off again. This time she was fifty-five.

Emilie had no outstanding debt, a little money saved, and a husband who continued to be gainfully employed. But she was stuck—unable to see that other options were available. She didn't have to keep looking and looking for a job in a field that was offering diminishing returns. Emilie again set about looking for a job "like it was a job." After another year of looking with few interviews and no prospects, Emilie sought advice from an old friend.

Her friend had been a banker for thirty years and had recently transitioned to running a not-for-profit venture-capital group. She advised Emilie to think about her skills in a different way—in a context beyond the actual work she had been doing, to separate the skills from the situation. By doing this, Emilie realized that her organizational abilities and service orientation might have another life. And that one of her assets was a Rolodex of highly placed executives at a broad array of companies. As a result of much targeted inquiry, one of her previous clients helped her find a place in a small entrepreneurial organization located right near Emilie's home. "I haven't been this happy or this appreciated in a decade!" Emilie told us.

> **Paula:** Emilie's story ultimately had a happy ending, but it took getting fired twice and some very good advice from a friend to help her see that the trajectory of her career had peaked.
>
> **Jeff:** The most positive part of the story, however, was that she was able to capitalize on her decades of experience in a new way and create an entirely new career for herself. Unfortunately, we met many boomers who stay in the same rut—and essentially dig their own grave.
>
> **Paula:** That's classic stuck—pursuing a very restricted course of action even when you know the odds of a good outcome are very small. Getting fired is an invitation to look not just at your goals but also at your own professional assets and liabilities. They may have changed since the last time

you looked. And at least consider the possibility that you may have got what was coming to you. You know, there is a cruel justice to the business world. Sometimes getting fired is a mercy killing.

Jeff: It bears mentioning that almost everyone we spoke with who got fired or laid off ultimately believed it was the best thing that ever happened to him or her.

Paula: But it often took a lot of time in a pain cave to create a new solution.

"The best thing I got from my job in finance was a lot of frequent-flier points," Pete told us. "We had regional offices in four cities, and I went to each one at least once a month, going over the books and the P & L [profit and loss] and accounts receivable. I worked at the same company for over ten years. We imported paper products. It was OK, but mostly I liked the people and I thought they liked me. So when I got downsized and replaced with a videoconference machine, I thought there would be this outburst of rage from the people I worked with. Maybe they would go on strike and demand that they hire me back. There was nothing. 'Sorry about that,' was as much as I got. They were just glad it wasn't them.

"I truly was lost. I'd been divorced for almost five years, so there wasn't a lot of sympathy there. 'I hope you can still afford child support,' was my ex-wife's first comment. And my girlfriend had other things on her mind, as well: 'We can't get married until you get a new job.' I didn't remember actually asking her.

"After I spent a couple of weeks trying to find another accounting job that would solve everybody's problems, it just came to me: What do I want? What would make *me* happy? I had absolutely no idea. So—and here's where the frequent flier miles come in—I flew to Costa Rica all by myself. Probably the first vacation alone that I'd ever had. And I took diving lessons. Really. I'd never been diving before in my life. And I know this sounds crazy, but I fell in love with it. I hung out at the dive shop every day. The owner offered me a job (for very little money, by the way). And four months later, I owned the shop. I never wanted to own a store or a business of any kind. Now I own a dive shop in Costa Rica. I love saying that: 'I own a dive shop in Costa Rica.' I love everything about it. I am cosmically happy for the first time in my life."

> **Jeff:** Although we met very few dive-shop owners, many boomers start their own businesses or become independent contractors in their fifties. The autonomy and control they have seems to far outweigh the risk and even, in many cases, the reduced income.
>
> **Paula:** Autonomy, control, and no more wondering if they will be the next one to get laid off. There is no overestimating the level of fear and stress we heard from many of the boomers we spoke with. It starts at about forty-five and escalates from there.

Boomers have become the most self-employed generation in history—fully 30 percent claiming that job title, a number that is increasing every year.[11] Bruce Tulgan, a consultant on generational workplace issues, estimates that 3.5 million people between the ages of forty and fifty-eight vanished from the American workforce from 2001 to 2004. That's about 5 percent of all baby boomers.[12] Many of these people may have simply chosen to call themselves "self-employed" rather than "unemployed." Mark Zandi, chief economist at Economy.com, explains why losing a corporate job is harder on boomers: "Older white collar workers quickly become disenfranchised. They have difficulty getting back into the job market and when they do, their compensation is often significantly reduced."[13] Forty-five percent of all workers earn less money in a new job after being displaced—and this figure is significantly higher among the over forty-five population.[14]

> **Paula:** That sounds grim.
>
> **Jeff:** The numbers are pretty clear—if you get laid off or fired after fifty, you will have great difficulty finding comparable employment. You are likely to have better results by creating a new job or new career on your own.

Not only are older workers more likely to be self-employed, but they are also more likely to have a range of alternative work arrangements—part-time, on-call, independent contractors or the new, not always legal, category of "perm-a-lance," a freelance employee who is hired on a permanent basis—without benefits.[15]

Sometimes it isn't external events that motivate change, but a change in the way we feel about ourselves. Identity is a fluid concept. When work is part of our self-definition, sometimes we outgrow the jobs that fit better when we were younger.

Ronald Reagan reportedly said, "Some people spend an entire lifetime wondering if they made a difference. Marines don't have that problem." Most of us aren't marines, and we are concerned with the purpose of our lives in different ways at different life stages. A very large number of boomers are finding their work less satisfying than it once was and would like to do something different—if they could only figure out what.

Eric's work as a legal aid attorney defined him for nearly three decades. It was worth all the financial sacrifice and long hours because Eric felt that his work was giving his life a sense of purpose and that he was doing some real good. "Legal services provided me the chance to represent migrants, victims of domestic violence, seniors, classes of people who had been discriminated against in employment or housing. I also acted as a lobbyist to influence the law itself and help improve government programs."

But as time went on, Eric's point of view changed, and so did his feeling that what he was doing was making an important difference. "I started to first think seriously about leaving in 1996, when federal funding was slashed and the government implemented a number of very strict and unwanted regulations about what legal services could and could not do. I talked with the biggest firm in Seattle and was very close to accepting its offer, which would have increased my salary by fifty percent. I decided not to do that, because of the duress that legal services was in and because I couldn't imagine myself litigating in a big firm. But as time went on, it became more and more apparent that I was burning out.

"It took a few years for me to start really looking at alternatives. I realized that not only had legal services changed, but I had changed, too. I was sick of being at the mercy of the political climate. I wanted more free time, and I really wanted to save some money so that retirement could become a tangible possibility down the road. I started to look at opportunities that I wouldn't have considered a few years back. As it turned out, something did turn up that fit my requirements. And as luck would have it, they were looking for someone with a back-ground in public service. So I applied and got the job—I'm a very good interview. The work is easy, and mostly, I'm happier. I'm saving money for my retirement, and this job facilitates that in a way that legal services just couldn't."

Eric was able to see that work had a different purpose in his life now than when he was much younger. It took some time and a lot of soul searching, but ultimately, he saw that he had options—and he took advantage of them.

> **Paula:** Eric redeployed his skills—from the public sector to the private sector—which was un-usual. Most of the people we met went the other way. But his evaluation process could be a model for so many of us. He realized that his work with legal services was no longer giving him what he needed on any dimension.
>
> **Jeff:** His work no longer made him feel good about himself—and his concern about money for retirement became more urgent. But most of all, he was able to see that he had skills that he could use in another way.

Josh took a new route without a lot of advance planning: "The printing business was the family business. My grandfather was a printer's apprentice when he first came to America in 1900 and eventually started his own company. My very first job on my own was printing a book for a big insurance company. They paid me thirty thousand dollars; I printed the book for seventeen thousand—and I got to keep the difference. I thought, 'This is easy.' Of course, that was the last easy job I ever worked on."

The Internet dramatically changed the printing business almost overnight. When his three biggest clients left to print their own materials in-house, Josh was in a bind. He took a job at another printing company in New Jersey.

"I lasted two days and three hours. It was just not for me. Suit, tie, five bosses, sitting at a desk all day, working for somebody else. You can't imagine how liberated I felt as I walked to my car in the parking lot on that final day."

Then what? Josh had worked in the Flatiron district of Manhattan for over twenty-five years and had been a frequent diner at Eisenberg's Sandwich Shop, a local landmark. He got to know the owner, Steve, and they had joked about opening a restaurant together. But conversations had never progressed beyond casual banter over a bagel.

Josh, then fifty-one, made a life-changing decision. From the parking lot in New Jersey, he drove straight to Eisenberg's and told Steve he wanted to buy the restaurant. Then he went to the bank to borrow as much money as he could. He spent a month completing "Eisenbergs's Crash Course in Restaurant Management" with Steve—and has been at the front counter every day since. Josh still serves the classic corned beef and matzo ball soup and writes take-out orders on the bag it will be packed in—just as Steve had taught him to do.

"I was made for this business. I love schmoozing. I enjoy people, and I touch their lives. I feel engaged with them. And the best part is that I'm passionate about something. I haven't felt that way in years. I used to think that food was *like* sex. Now that I'm older, I think that food *is* sex."

That was in 2005, and his life has never been the same. "When I started, I had no idea what was involved. None. It's not the same on the other side of the counter." The restaurant business is extremely difficult, but Josh doesn't seem to mind. "You asked me about regrets? I have none. Well, maybe one. I wish I had bought this place sooner. Maybe five or ten years ago, when I was younger and had more energy. And I would like to put my own stamp on a place, but my customers would kill me if I changed the tuna-salad recipe."

> **Paula:** I love this story. And the sandwiches at Eisenberg's are the best in New York City. Josh did take the "leap" that Sara Davidson talks about in her book.[16] And for him, the net appeared.
>
> **Jeff:** Sometimes it makes sense to continue pursuing the goals we chose in our youth—and sometimes it just doesn't. No one wants to stay too long at the fair. But it can be hard to identify what time is the right time for a change.
>
> **Paula:** I have nothing but admiration for people who are able to make a plan and stick to it—but I am by nature a "leaper."
>
> **Jeff:** Planner or leaper—either alternative can be good. However, standing still is unlikely to have a good outcome.

For twenty-five years, Sam had been in banking, working at Wachovia and its predecessor companies. By fifty-four, Sam had reached nearly the highest levels of his industry as senior vice president/managing director of Global Markets and Wealth Management.

Every year, he got a little more money and a little more responsibility. "Keep your head up and keep moving forward" was his motto. Sam liked his job well enough; he had earned sufficient money to put his two kids through college and make retirement possible. But he knew that there was much more he could be doing and feeling. So when Wachovia offered early retirement to hundreds of executives (due to its merger with another bank), Sam took it.

Sam had several offers to move to another major financial institution in a similar position. But he said no to all of them. He had no plans, and his friends said he was crazy. What the hell was he going to do all day long? Sam was happily married to Isabelle, his wife of many years, and loved his house in Atlanta—no upheaval there. His kids were doing well and not likely to need more than a little assistance now and then. What could possibly fill his days?

Sam did not panic. At first, he focused on philanthropic work, temporarily taking over the executive director position of the Atlanta Ballet. But that wasn't his true passion—and he knew it. He stayed open to opportunities. "I told everyone I met that I was looking for something interesting to do. I guess that was my secret. When I first retired, I felt obligated to tell people how busy I was. 'I'm busier now than I was when I was working' seems to be the mantra of the recently retired. That's what you are supposed to say, but I wasn't that busy. I had plenty of time to try new things. And I wasn't shy about telling people that."

Through mutual friends, he met a man who was starting a global microfinance fund. Sam jumped all over it. "This opportunity never would have come along if I had still been working at Wachovia. I needed some time to open myself to something like this."

And that's what Sam is doing today—providing funding for microfinance institutions, which in turn make $50 and $100 loans to impoverished people around the world—small business owners for whom that can mean the difference between hunger and an education for their kids. Sam does not believe that this will be the last career change he will make. And if you believe career coaches, who say that four to seven careers is the average, Sam has a couple more to go. "I'm not looking for that one perfect career. I know my life will be filled with a whole patchwork of new opportunities. And I am looking forward to every single one."

Paula: My own experience was similar to Sam's—though much less orderly. I quit my job without a plan. I knew I could get another job in advertising, but I hoped to find something new. But what? I didn't have a clue. I felt stuck.

After a few months of drifting, I did one deliberate thing: I decided that I would put myself in the way of new things and new people. I really only knew people in the ad business. And I figured that if I wanted to do something different, I had to get beyond my usual circle. Somehow, talking to the many successful professional people I knew through the industry just wasn't ringing any bells. So I decided that for six months, I would do *anything* anyone asked me to do that was outside my usual routine—especially if it sounded like something I would hate—just as an exercise in opening myself to new experiences.

Which is how I found myself on a Department of Corrections bus to Rikers Island prison on a snowy day with about ten other women. Everyone except the woman who invited me was a complete stranger. All the women were about the same age as I was, so the bus conversation was about grown kids and menopause and what to do next. I volunteered as little information as humanly possible, but the women were very persistent. I had been introduced as a former ad exec, and they all wanted to know what I wanted to do. Only because I felt that I had to say something, I said that I was thinking I might want to teach. "Teach what—advertising?" "Oh no," I said. I was sure of that. If I were going to think about ads, I'd just as soon make them. But I do have a dusty old PhD in sociology. Within two weeks, through a friend of a friend of someone on the bus, I was teaching Intro Sociology at a small liberal arts college in the Berkshires.

Jeff: You and Sam put yourselves in the way of opportunity. If you get out of your usual circles and alert others to your interest in trying new things, new options are more likely to occur. And you have to ask for help, tell people what you need. Emilie got a push from her banker friend; Sam told everyone he knew he was looking for something new.

Paula: I think it is also important to consider that the first thing you try might not be the right thing. It wasn't for me or for Sam. I taught for about five years and then moved on. Sam ran an arts organization until an opportunity that interested him more showed up.

Jeff: And you have to be able to recognize the next new thing when it shows up—that means keeping your head up and your eyes open.

Paula: Career advisers say it takes two to six years to make a midlife career transition. Our evidence is that this seems to be about right.

What About Retirement?

What do we mean by retirement, anyway? Eighty percent of boomers say they will work well past sixty-five, and about half say they will work well into their seventies.[17] It's only been in the past few decades that healthy people have stopped working for the last twenty or thirty years of their lives.

Retirement didn't exist in an agrarian society. Men and women worked until they could physically work no longer. The industrial revolution made it possible for some to work past what had been considered a "productive" age. Retirement was fabricated by the British government in the late 1880s as a way to reduce the number of older workers and to make way for younger members to join the workforce. It was not an altruistic invention, merely a means to increase efficiency, which was of growing importance in an industrialized society.[18]

Retirement gained widespread acceptance in America, especially during the Great Depression. The government encouraged older workers to get out of the way and make room for younger ones. In 1920, the U.S. Civil Service introduced mandatory retirement age with a minimal pension. The presumption was that after the age of sixty-five, financial requirements were modest. If necessary, the aged could live with younger relatives.

After the Social Security Act was signed in 1935, the notion of retirement as a right and reward began to take root in the American psyche. The period following World War II saw the fastest increase in retirement due to the expansion of the social security program, the growth of corporate pension plans, and intensive marketing by insurance companies and, later, brokerage firms, that managed pension plans according to government law. The creation of "retirement" was a masterful marketing phenomenon but not necessarily a workable economic idea. This is an urgent consideration as the most populous generation in history comes of age.

For several years, economists have been alarmed at the thought of seventy-five million people—that's 26 percent of the U.S. population—leaping into the traditional retirement paradigm. That could mean seventy-five million people living for another twenty-five or thirty years with little or no income. In 2000, there were 3.4 employed workers contributing to social security for every person over the age of sixty-five. By 2030, that number would drop precipitously to only two workers for every recipient of social security. This unintended consequence was unanticipated by the original legislation.

Social security was initially devised to pay for nearly all the expenses of the lowest-income recipients. Today, the program continues to fund the bulk of a retiree's living expenses—constituting more than half the income for 60 percent of the program's beneficiaries and more than 90 percent of the income for 30 percent of the program's recipients.[19] Working adults today have a far lower expectation of the future of social security. Most boomers believe that it will account for less than one-third of their retirement income.[20] This expectation is a far cry from social security's first recipient, who paid $22.54 into the system and received $22,000 in benefits.[21]

> **Jeff:** To a large degree, retirement may be a social experiment that has outlived its usefulness. For white-collar professionals, work provides the primary form of social capital. As we have discussed, retirement means to give up a large part of one's identity.
>
> **Paula:** *Retirement* literally means a period of withdrawal—to back away from activity. There is a crushing finality even to the word itself. It is a destination—the one that comes before death.
>
> **Jeff:** It has often meant an increased dependence on others. It may mean a loss of self-confidence, especially for the men and women of the baby-boom generation who have unabashedly drawn much of their feelings of self-worth from their careers.
>
> **Paula:** We met a number of people who flunked traditional retirement for all sorts of reasons.

The identity issue is a powerful one. Bonnie had been a pioneer: a member of that small subset of working women who really did do it all. She had many setbacks and many career successes and was, above all else, resilient. She had two children and a fulfilling marriage and even managed some board work, on the side. "I loved it all," she told us, "the highs, the lows, and everything in between." Bonnie was known for her energy and enthusiasm, but after thirty years, it literally wore her out.

When her company offered early retirement, she jumped at it. She figured she could spend a year just cleaning her closets.

It was a nice thought, but Bonnie, who seldom shed a tear, was weeping all the time. This will pass, she thought. But it didn't. Her husband tried to comfort her—he was actually delighted to have her more available to him—but Bonnie missed the camaraderie of the workplace. She made an effort to see friends, though they were still working and had little time. While Bonnie understood, she was very unhappy. She went to museums and movies and was more available to her ailing mother and her high-school-aged kids. Meanwhile, however, her self-confidence eroded with every passing month.

Bonnie had not anticipated the degree to which her sense of self-worth was connected to her work. "It's not that I want to go back to the company—I don't think I could physically do it anymore. But I feel like I've lost my sense of purpose. There is no reason to get up in the morning. When I was going to work the whole effing show would stop if I wasn't there. Now, it simply doesn't matter. I so miss that rush."

Out of desperation, Bonnie volunteered to teach English as a second language (ESL) to adults. "Helping the new immigrant population seemed worthwhile. I really believed that speaking English would make a difference for them. I just had to do something. I was drowning." Within three months, Bonnie had revamped the curriculum. Within six months, she was running the program. At the one-year mark, she had converted the volunteer job into a part-time paid position administering a number of community programs.

As is her way, Bonnie has thrown herself into this job, taking on every aspect, from rearranging the furniture, to mentoring young volunteers—and even her boss. Bonnie has found herself again. "I sucked at retirement," she told us. "I really sucked at it. Never did anything as poorly as I did that one. If retirement was a job, I would have been fired the first week."

> **Paula:** Purpose means a couple of things as we age and as we contemplate a change in work status. For some, like Eric, work was a life Purpose with a capital *P*, not just a lifestyle. It was a calling. For many others, our job provided purpose with a small *p*: The job provided the outline of the day and the year—busy seasons, slow seasons, vacations, and other rhythms of daily life. The thought of being without that definition feels like dissolving into a puddle on the floor without shape or form.
>
> **Jeff:** The anxiety is really about the unknown. We don't know what we don't know—that's the good news and the bad news.

Jack is naturally an intellectually curious person; one could say he was a problem solver by birth. And he loved his work. After many years at a well-known and highly esteemed consultancy, he started a consulting company of his own. Ten years of hard work with a dozen talented partners built the company to one thousand employees in eight countries. He and his colleagues sold it for a price he had only dreamed of. For him, the financial issue was taken care of. He moved to Florida and bought a house on a golf course. That move lasted less than two years.

Jack remained Jack—intellectually curious. Florida didn't scratch his itch. He missed the diversity of views his former company had provided him with, and he missed the problem solving. So he moved back to New York. His Hourglass Solution was a new consultancy—smaller in scale with different objectives—but it continues to allow him to do something he loves and retain his connections in a field of work in which he had spent a lifetime developing skills.

Larry also had trouble with traditional retirement. As one of the earliest boomers, Larry turned sixty in 2005 and saw this birthday as permission to retire from his successful career as a magazine editor in New York City. The sale of his co-op and the purchase of a home in Boca Raton followed quickly— almost as quickly as there arose an intense boredom and the realization that he had made a terrible mistake. "I didn't think it would be a problem," he told us. "I thought I'd just freelance." He discovered that it was not so easy. Florida and other traditional retirement destinations are filled with people who intend to use their skills as freelancers and consultants. The demand just isn't there. At sixty-one, Larry returned to New York, having vowed not to make the same mistake twice. At last report, Larry was still looking for a way to get back into the business.

> **Paula:** Traditional retirement is tough for a lot of boomers—"Who am I now that I don't work?" Many described the feeling of discomfort when asked, "What do you do?" For years after I left advertising, I wanted to answer, "Well, I used to be Paula Forman."
>
> **Jeff:** And Larry had other problems—boredom and isolation. He was used to the companionship and stimulation of the office and found it very difficult to replace either one on an ad hoc basis.

Jeff: We found a lot more people who had trouble with retirement than we expected. The first few months of giddy indulgences gave rise to boredom and depression and ever-diminishing sense of self.

Paula: Many people we talked to had retired expecting that they would easily redeploy their skills in the not-for-profit sector. Most were not as fortunate as Bonnie. Although board positions or volunteer work sometimes is a possibility, the not-for-profit sector is not waiting with bated breath for those who have been involved in commerce to take their jobs.

Jeff: Yes, these organizations were happy to have retirees write a check, attend events, volunteer to help. But actual jobs were much harder to come by. We boomers are defeated by our numbers again. There are simply not enough paid positions at charitable organizations to accommodate the hoards who want to "give back."

Boomers are volunteering in record numbers: 30 percent versus less than 25 percent for the so-called Greatest Generation.[22] But boomers are not finding it nearly as gratifying as they had anticipated. Nearly one-third fail to return for a second year.[23] Expecting to use their skills and experience in a philanthropic way, the volunteers often find themselves licking envelopes instead. "Boomers are a fussy bunch," say Suzanne Perry and Michael Aft in an analysis of boomer volunteers, "and charities need to learn how to accommodate them. They want positions where they can make a difference, research shows, and most nonprofit groups have not figured out how to offer them those kinds of opportunities."[24]

Jeff: These retirement and volunteer issues are yet another indication that for boomers, the search for personal fulfillment doesn't come to a screeching halt at fifty.

Paula: Retirement has as many different permutations and combinations as there are people. Successful retirement for boomers requires some planning, but, most of all, great flexibility—and the willingness to consider significant change.

Jeff: A lot of the boomers we talked to planned to be consultants or freelancers or—the most popular retirement career of all—teachers. Unfortunately, you're probably more likely to get a job as a greeter at Wal-Mart than you are to get a paid job as a teacher. A bitter pill for many.

Paula: On the other hand, we did find many retired boomers who were excited by what they were doing, optimistic about their future, and, in fact, having the greatest adventure of their lives. But to a person, they had made some big changes. Many of these people moved, not necessarily in the traditional paths to warmer climates. Some moved from the suburbs to urban areas; some from urban to rural counties. Some downsized; others reallocated resources. Their stories may inspire you.

Mark had just turned fifty when he was fired from the job he had held since he had graduated from college. He and his wife, Stella, had chosen not to have kids and divided their time between Manhattan and their house in Berkshire County.

When Mark was fired, they were shocked, embarrassed, and scared. It was totally unanticipated and, in their minds, a disaster. They considered suing his employer. Mark looked for another job—almost feverishly. He took every freelance assignment he was offered, although he had a long and generous severance package. Each freelance position was more irritating than the last and only exacerbated his panic. Mark was moody and irascible, so much so that Stella "retired" to the country for some relief.

Then, as Mark described it, he had a life-changing revelation. As he was preparing his taxes, he realized that with his pension, savings, and miscellaneous investments, they "had enough" money to live reasonably comfortably—anyplace in the world but New York City. They were far from wealthy, and they had nowhere near the grand total they had hoped to have by retirement age. But they knew they could get by.

It took them all of a month to pack up and move to the Berkshires full time, pocketing some extra cash from the sale of their apartment. The only plan they made was a solemn promise to each other to spend several months every winter traveling and never to work again.

The first winter they spent in Italy. They rented a small and very inexpensive house in Sienna and spent several weeks in Venice as well. It was fun, but they didn't love it. The second year, they rented a funky and, again, inexpensive apartment in Paris right on Boulevard Saint-Michel, just a block from the Île Saint-Louis. This was more like what they had had in mind.

They rented in Paris again the following year and decided to buy a tiny place on the Rue d l'Ancienne Comédie, in the heart of the Left Bank. It was an adventure. They enjoyed every minute of furnishing that place—exclusively from flea markets. Mark described their time there as idyllic. "The only thing we ever argued about was who got to carry the bread home."

Their residence in Paris inspired many of their friends to visit. And those who didn't, wished they had. Stella and Mark made a Parisian life for themselves. They studied French, Stella took a course in French cooking, and they spent their afternoons in the cafés around their apartment with their dogs, Ralph and Alice.

Paris was defining for this couple. It was more than another home—it defined their life stage. It was the Paris/Berkshires period. It affected everything, from the smallest issues of fashion to the way they thought of themselves. Retirement enabled them to become cosmopolitans in a way they had never been in New York.

Mark reflects on their transformation: "Getting fired was the best thing that could have happened to me. I would have continued in the same rut, hating it more every year. I already hated it—I just didn't know how to quit. It was a lucky break. It forced us to make choices and it changed our lives." Not surprisingly, then, when Stella and Mark tired of Paris, they sold their apartment and built a house in Mexico. They had learned the rhythm of choice.

Other moves were not as dramatic but yielded just as happy outcomes. Ed and Stephanie had both been deeply involved in music. In their youth, Stephanie had performed at Carnegie Hall and Ed played with a jazz trio. But long before they turned thirty, the demands of their work and family life took precedence. They had three children and a house in the suburbs, and both worked in a family textile business. It wasn't a passion, but it made them rich enough. When their children were grown and left home, Ed and Stephanie took off as well. "New Jersey was just over," Stephanie said. They sold the house and the business and headed for Manhattan.

Retirement for them means going out nearly every night of the week. They love cabaret and are well known at the clubs around town and, on occasion, can be persuaded to perform. They are board members of a thriving off-off-Broadway theater and have expanded their group of friends and interests. Their love of music and esteem for performers became the basis for a new lifestyle and self-image. When they retired, they moved thirty miles—and light-years—away.

Like Ed and Stephanie, Mathew used a career and job transition to reorient his life around something that he loved: the sport of lacrosse. Mat had gone to public school on Long Island, where he first learned to play lacrosse, in the fourth grade. He was a star player in high school and was heavily recruited at many of the top college programs in the country. He earned an MBA from New York University and had a successful career as a brand manager in a number of different consumer-goods categories—from soup to paper towels. Ultimately, he started his own company designing and manufacturing specialty packaging for high-end retail stores and cosmetic companies.

The lure of lacrosse never went away. He played club lacrosse after college and started a lacrosse team at the New Jersey high school where he had been a teacher for three years. Later, while raising a family in New York City, he founded the first-ever youth lacrosse program in that city. He also stayed involved in the national development of the game, serving in several executive committee positions with U.S. Lacrosse, the sport's governing body.

In 2003, he merged his packaging business with a larger competitive company and signed a three-year contract. That's when the plan started to fall into place. He loved to teach, he was a great coach, he knew how to start and build a business, and he knew how to run a sports program—and he knew that U.S. Lacrosse had broadened its mission to bring lacrosse to the inner cities of America. His dream was to develop lacrosse as a mainstream sport for urban kids in New York and its schools.

He developed a business plan for a public/private partnership, took it to the Department of Education's Public School Athletic League, and got it approved. "Most people think of lacrosse as an upper-class, preppy, suburban, white man's sport played at elite northeastern schools and colleges. One rung below polo. I wanted kids in Harlem, the Bronx, Brooklyn, and Queens to have the same opportunities that I had through lacrosse. If some of these kids got involved in the sport, it might open up some new doors for them."

After two years of working through the bureaucracy of the New York City public school system "selling the game," fundraising, begging, borrowing, and even investing his own money, his not-for-profit company, City LAX, Inc., was born. Today, over five hundred kids from eighteen public high schools participate in City LAX–assisted programs. "I've gone from a hefty paycheck every week to being much more careful about my personal finances. Sometimes, this can be stressful. But I have incredible support from my wife and kids, and I believe I'm making a difference as a social entrepreneur. Lacrosse is a special game that has given me great pleasure and opportunities. People talk to me like I'm some big philanthropist making a huge sacrifice. That's a little embarrassing. I believe that what I'm doing is a good thing, but I'm also doing it for me. Sharing my love for this sport makes me happy every single day."

Mat achieved his Hourglass Solution by looking at everything he loved to do and everything he was good at. He took apart his life, looked at what was valuable to him now, for the present and for the future, and put the pieces back together in a new combination.

> **Paula:** Successful retirement for most seems to require taking a risk of some sort.
>
> **Jeff:** It apparently isn't sufficient for most people just to do more of a thing you've always enjoyed—like golf or gardening. The affinity needs to be transformed from a passive pursuit into something with a plan. For people who have spent their working lives making something happen, the most successful retirees are those who continue to have an impact. The arena may change, but the desire to make a difference in some way doesn't seem to.
>
> **Paula:** The relationship between identifying options and the ability to make change is also apparent. One thing does lead to another. People who identify choices and act on them find new options. It is a kind of cosmic flexibility. People who are flexible enough to make one change seem to develop an appetite for it.
>
> **Jeff:** Another factor is the ability to make mistakes and take them in stride. Many of the people

we talked with—in fact, the majority of people who were now quite satisfied with their work decisions or with retirement—had tried other options that hadn't provided the perfect solution. Some tried traditional retirement and changed their minds. Others, like you and Sam, tried different kinds of work until the right thing came along.

Paula: And of course, persistence. The optimum Hourglass Solution is highly personal and may evolve over time or present itself serendipitously as it did for Josh. The answer isn't easy for anyone. But it does seem clear that the willingness to take some risk, the understanding that mistakes are part of the process, and flexibility in both vision and execution is a good recipe for Greater Adulthood.

7

Our Money:
Rethinking Dollars and Sense

Boomers have grown up in a time of unprecedented prosperity. Although there have been many recessions, the overall economic outlook has been positive for their entire lives. The Depression of 1929 is a distant historical and impersonal event. Boomers have spent their whole working lives during the economically strongest period in U.S. history. Until now. It may be that boomers are the least prepared of all to handle the current economic climate.

Because of the exponential rise in disposable funds, most boomers plowed a substantial portion of their yearly income into lifestyle improvements. They lived large, bought big cars, big houses, and big TVs. Boomers now control 70 percent of the wealth in this country and account for about half of all spending, buying over two trillion dollars' worth of goods and services every year.

Missing from this rosy picture are a few more details. Boomers are in terrible debt. Credit-card liability has grown

from $238 billion in 1998 to $952 billion in 2008, dispropor-
tionately due to boomer spending.[1] And the average boomer
family saw its debt grow 33 percent from 2001 to 2004.[2]

And boomers are not savers. Unlike their parents' generation, spending—not saving—has been a way of life. For the
previous generation, for whom the Depression was still vivid,
saving was an important element in their feelings of optimism
and security for the future. Saving made them feel good. Deferred gratification was a point of pride.

Not so for boomers. Baby boomers have done less financial
planning for the future than previous generations did. Even
though they are much more likely to live in a two-income
household and have more disposable income, boomers have a
much lower savings rate. The year 2007 was the third consecutive "negative savings year" for boomers—the first time this has
happened since the 1930s. That means that as a group, they
continue to spend more than they earned. Almost 28 percent of
all boomers have savings of less than $10,000, not counting the
value of their primary residence. Over 60 percent have saved less
than $100,000.[3]

Exacerbating the problem is that social security and
Medicare, safety nets for the two previous generations, have
uncertain prospects for boomers. Even guaranteed pensions, a
staple of corporate America for decades, covers only 16 percent
of the workforce.[4] Again, the pig in the python—the sheer size
of the boomer population—is the culprit. These programs were
not designed to handle a generation that is seventy-five million
strong, nor to operate under conditions in which retirees might
actually outnumber the contributing workforce.

To a large degree, boomers put their money into their
homes. While the average household size decreased by one per-

son from 1950 to today, the average home size doubled, and no country has as many bathrooms per person as America does.[5] This investment may have offset the lack of savings in previous years, but the sudden decline in home values in 2008 has put a kink in many boomers' plans. Ten million U.S. homeowners, in fact, have a negative home value.[6]

The high-debt and low-savings profile for boomers is not necessarily about profligate spending. Although some boomer critics have practiced rants about overconsumption and a predilection for self-indulgence, this is an incomplete picture. The steady rise in the price of home ownership and the concurrent deregulation of credit, the failure of the public school system and the exorbitant costs of private education on both a secondary and college level, the skyrocketing cost of medical insurance and medical care, and a job market that no longer protects employees are the hard facts.

Boomers now outsource to the private sector much of what previous generations did for themselves or the government did for them. We pay for our kids to be educated, our parents to be taken care of, our dogs to be walked, and our homes to be cleaned, in part because of a breakdown in the systems discussed above but also because of the time crunch of the two-income family. Studies have consistently shown that a second income may actually result in a lower standard of living and greater financial jeopardy.[7]

The macroeconomic picture for boomers needs some urgent attention. Adjustments can and will be made on all levels, including those that the government has postponed for far too long. Nevertheless, microadjustments need to be made as well. Greater Adulthood is about control, and nothing, next to physical health, is more enabling than money. But our choices for the future can also be constrained by our ideas about money. Our financial obligations may be a product of decisions that no longer work as well as they did when the obligations were undertaken. Or unexpected financial burdens may seem to have usurped our choices. Perhaps the financial goal we had in mind served a life that is no longer relevant. This chapter is about sorting our way through this very complex issue.

Jeff: Money enables choice and is a real, and sometimes not-so-real, stumbling block for boomers who are trying to create their Hourglass Solution. It often becomes a failsafe rationale for people who are unwilling or unable to look at alternatives.

Paula: In our culture, "I need the money" is a conversation stopper. It is the rare friend who will question assumptions about how much money you say you need, or why you need it. But the phrase "I need the money" is often an indication that the player is stuck and hasn't found a way to talk about that feeling—or even think about it. The comments we heard were not subtle:

"I am still in this damn job because I don't have the dough to retire!"

"I'd love to try something else, but nothing pays like the job I have."

"I'd love to chuck it all and move to someplace warm—but we just can't swing it financially."

"We just don't have enough money yet."

Jeff: We heard dozens of people talk about their options as though the choices were completely determined by their financial situations. It is easy to know precisely what we can't afford. It is very difficult, however, to push beyond the very real constraints presented by our bank accounts and look at what alternatives we can afford.

Paula: We have all grown accustomed to a certain style of life—whatever it is. Most of us are very hesitant to rearrange the pieces of our life or to look at other options. "We just don't have the money" can be a statement of fact, but it is also a statement of stuck.

Jeff: The problem requires great specificity to break it apart. Just what don't you have the money for?

Cultural attitudes about money are deeply embedded, and our personal views are hardwired as well. Judgments about sufficiency and excess are simply that—judgments—and vary by ethnicity and class. One of the first hurdles a new couple must surmount is attitudes about money. It is inevitable that any two people will have had different formative experiences. Every new life stage is an opportunity to refine these attitudes and practices.

As children, we were subject to our parents' views about money. Mom and dad told us in subtle and not-so-subtle ways about the importance of money and appropriate levels of consumption and saving. In young adulthood, we accept or reject or evolve those ideas as we wish. We build a lifestyle by making choices. Income and expectations are qualifiers of those choices. What is easy to forget is that lifestyle is a choice, not an obligation. Greater Adulthood provides the opportunity to refine or perhaps change course.

Bill says he feels anxious every time a discussion of retirement and money for the future arises—even though he has been putting money in a 401(k) for twenty-five years and has many other assets. "I guess we could do other things, but I feel too upset to talk about it with my wife. She always starts the conversation with 'I don't want to sell the house,' so that ends the discussion right there. I just feel anxious. I would like to work less, but I think if we had less money, it would, you know, create problems. We probably would have to make changes. Carol doesn't understand how much our life costs, and I don't think she could change."

Bill doesn't know what he is afraid of. Perhaps he fears that others will perceive a change at this stage as an admission of failure. Perhaps he feels that it is a failure. And yet he knows—whether he has the vocabulary or not—that he is *stuck*. Stuck in a life that he created long ago but that has ceased to be nourishing to him.

"How much is enough?" Louis asked everyone that question when he left his lucrative job at a hedge fund. Interestingly, most of his peers had roughly the same answer—and almost everyone was more than a little short of the arbitrary goal.

"It didn't seem to matter how much money these guys had. They always felt they had to keep doing what they were doing because they didn't have enough to retire." Louis observed that no one ever questioned the number, except to raise it. The game was to accumulate more and more, and the thought of rearranging the pieces and living with what they already had was an admission of weakness—or failure.

That bumper sticker from the 1980s—"The person who dies with the most toys wins"—became politically incorrect by the 1990s, but many boomers didn't get the message. Traditionally, the spending patterns of senior citizens became more conservative. As they "retired" from society, they earned less and spent less. Their discretionary funds were often used to help children and grandchildren. Baby boomers have turned this pattern upside down. Instead of spending less as they get older, boomers are spending more. In fact, as boomers age, they tend to spend more and more on themselves with each passing year. The average member of a fifty-plus household spends nineteen thousand dollars per year; this is 30 percent more than the average member of an under-fifty household.[8]

- A typical boomer will buy thirteen cars in his or her life-time—seven of those purchases taking place after the age of fifty.[9]

- Female consumers between the ages of fifty-five and sixty-four spent more per capita on women's apparel than did any other age group—$788 annually (in 2002).[10]

- AARP found that over half the buyers of a Harley-Davidson were over forty-five years old.

   Jeff: Boomers' inclination to buy things for themselves as they age may be an expression of satisfaction and pleasure. The stuff you buy may reflect the relative affluence that marks midlife, the rewards of a job well done and good planning.

Paula: The "shopping jones," however, can be as limiting as any other addiction. The need to make a lot of money to support a retail habit can keep you stuck in the neck of the hourglass.

Jeff: Spending is to some degree driven by your peers—and by your environment. It is hard to practice restraint when those around you are in the throes of retail madness.

Paula: Like living green in a world of energy abusers.

The issue for boomers in midlife is to evaluate the pattern of their own spending and determine the degree to which their money is enabling choice—or if their consumer choices are actually decreasing their options. In a culture that has defined *winners* as those who have accumulated the most stuff, the decision to alter that paradigm is life-changing. Money is a tool; decisions about how to use it can be a trigger to create greater choice and may catapult you into an Hourglass Solution of new dimension.

Financial issues need not be controlling. Our need for money, like so many of our other needs, is highly variable over a lifetime. When we are in our twenties, thirties, and forties, we are in a building phase. For some people, the building phase continues throughout their lives, but the requirement for cash may change. For most of us, the heavy-expense years pass when the last child is educated. That's a fine time to assess not just the state of one's finances, but also the evolution of one's attitudes about money. Not surprisingly, research has found that as we get older, "having a lot of money" becomes less and less a sign of success and accomplishment.

We need to rethink how and why we spend our money. Conservative columnist and author David Brooks believes that this may be the moral issue of the twenty-first century: "The country's moral guardians are forever looking for decadence out of Hollywood and reality TV. But the most rampant decadence today is financial decadence, the trampling of decent norms about how to use and harness money."[11]

Nearly half of a typical families' budget is spent on nonessential items.[12] The trend analysts at Iconoculture summed up America's penchant for gratuitous purchases: "Make a list of the last ten things you bought. If you're like most Americans, four of the items on your list are unnecessary—things you don't need, but just wanna have."[13]

The situation has gotten so out of control that an entire industry has sprung up to handle it: Self-storage units are a twenty-two-billion-dollar business growing 740 percent since the late 1980s.[14] Apparently, it takes forty-five thousand storage facilities across the United States to handle the stuff that Americans have bought but can't fit into their three-thousand-square-foot homes.

Roberta and Monty are an attractive and gregarious couple in their late fifties. They ran a successful Chicago business that provided an exotic lifestyle for themselves and their children for many years. They traveled widely, both for work and for pleasure, and have a trove of colorful stories and many trophies from that stage of their lives. When their last child left home, they did what they had promised themselves they would do for nearly a decade: They retired to live and work as artists.

They sold their expensive home and began their search for a new life. "We thought about moving to Europe and considered a number of locations in the U.S. We wanted an urban environment and a less expensive lifestyle," Monty told us. They moved to Saratoga, a small city in upstate New York with a special affection for the arts. That was six years ago.

They have bought and renovated two houses and sold them both at a profit. Though they work locally, they maintain a schedule that leaves ample time for Monty's sculpting and Roberta's painting. They have had several shows of their work and are highly visible contributors to their community and the social life of the town. "We lived large for so many years," Roberta told us recently from her part-time job at a local teahouse. "And now we live small and love it. We loved our life before. And we love our life now. I wouldn't give up either."

> **Paula:** In our own conversations with boomers, we found little correlation between the amount of money someone had and his or her ability to create options and make new choices. In other words, rich people were just as stuck as those who had much less money.
>
> **Jeff:** I was quite surprised that people with millions of dollars and those with very little savings were equally constrained in their thinking about options. Money was a significant roadblock for many, even in their ability to visualize alternatives.
>
> **Paula:** On the other hand, creative options exist at all income levels. There is no question that having a tidy nest egg after age fifty can be ex-

tremely helpful, but we talked to many people who found their Hourglass Solution without an inheritance or a trust fund.

Gabe and Nelda were fifty-five and fifty-three when they decided that Kansas was not where they were going to spend the rest of their lives. A couple of years before, they had rented an RV and took a trip to Florida. The trip would change their lives forever.

"I was working part-time at the post office in town, and Gabe was working at an auto parts store. A typical vacation for us was a fishing trip or a visit to the kids in Tulsa. When Gabe rented an RV for two weeks, I was excited and a little afraid. I wasn't sure if we could really spend two weeks all cooped up. It didn't turn out like that at all."

Even though it was summer, they drove to the Everglades, which they had always wanted to see. Their first night there, they hooked up the RV and treated themselves to dinner at the lodge. That's where they met Annie and Archie, who were of similar age and background and who were working in the restaurant—Annie as a hostess and Archie as a cook. As the four of them got to talking, Gabe and Nelda joked, "We should quit our jobs and work here, too." That's when they discovered that this is what many others had already done.

It turned out to be quite a system. The company that manages national park restaurants throughout the country hires hundreds of retirees and near-retirees who want to live in Florida for one season and Maine for another; or Arizona one year and Montana the next—mobility extends as far as the national parks. Whenever a park is open, there is plenty of work—all arranged in advance.

It took Gabe and Nelda two years to plan for the transition. And once it was done, there hasn't been a single regret. "In the three years we have been doing this, we've been to the Everglades twice, Acadia in Maine, the Grand Tetons, and Mount Rushmore. I would never have even seen those places. Both of us work about four or five hours a day. We get a free hook-up for our RV and enough money for just about anything we need. Don't forget—when you live in a trailer, you can't buy too much stuff. Gabe and I have kind of a system. Whenever we buy anything, other than food, we have to throw something out. It keeps me from buying too much junk in the souvenir shops."

Beyond the very creative solution discovered by Nelda and Gabe, boomers are finding new approaches to have fun—and not pay "retail." Barter has become a way of life for many, and Web sites like Craigslist have made it accessible to all—where piano lessons are traded for personal training and your house in Cincinnati is temporarily swapped for a two-week vacation apartment in Rome. As car sales decline, bike sales increase, as does fractional ownership of a host of big-ticket items. Even haggling is returning as a rediscovered art form.

People are constrained by many aspects of their financial situation. Some boomers, mostly men, felt confined by obligations to other family members. Their sense of self-worth was dependent upon their ability to provide a style of living for their wives and even adult children. Some boomers support their parents as well, and these obligations can make it seem as if there are no options. Many financially overloaded boomers have passionately insisted that they simply "have no choice." The dependent spouse, the daughter who is a single mother, the parents who have run out of savings, can all be financial drains and contribute to the feeling of being stuck with no choices. Obligations and responsibilities are highly personal and a product of many factors. We have no panacea for those who find themselves burdened with supporting others, except to insist that there are always options and choices to be made.

> **Jeff:** You owe yourself a hard assessment of your responsibilities to others. This is no different from an assessment of your consumer behavior.
>
> **Paula:** You may find that all other possibilities are simply unacceptable, or you may find that a modest revision can make a big difference. But the important thing is to recognize that there are choices—even in a situation that has been in place for years.
>
> **Jeff:** Much psychological and anecdotal evidence suggests that feeling that you have made a choice—as opposed to feeling trapped by a situation that is out of your control—makes an enormous difference in your outlook.

Think About Moving

One of the most significant aspects of stuck for so many people we spoke with was their commitment to a particular geographic location and often a particular piece of real estate. Has your home been an effective base for other activities? Is it still appropriate for what you want to do next? Perhaps the home you raised your family in is no longer necessary—but continues to be expensive. Downsizing is anathema to many boomers, but how about redefinition? For most, our homes are our largest equity. There is often considerable pressure to maintain the status quo, but great leverage is gained in changing it.

Theresa was geographically stuck. Though unemployed and without significant resources, she was completely unwilling to consider moving out of New York City, even though such a move might ease her financial worries considerably. A diehard Saks Fifth Avenue shopper and owner of sixteen Chanel cocktail dresses, she recognized that she was geographically rigid. "This act doesn't play outside New York City," she told us.

Other people we spoke with expressed interest in moving but insisted that they couldn't, because "the kids need to have us nearby" or "we want to be close to the grandkids" or "we should be near our folks" or simply "we've lived here forever." All these may be valid, but can play a role in aborting the decisions and challenges of Greater Adulthood. Making your house or your town or city a nonnegotiable element may severely limit the ability to redefine your options and make other choices.

In stark contrast, we found that the people who made a geographic move changed more than their address. Moving enabled other choices. For some people, moving was a way of "cleaning house" that repositioned them for a larger Hourglass Solution. Although *downsizing* is not a word most boomers like to contemplate, those who do generally find the process and the experience liberating. In a business context, the most enduring and potentially creative outcomes of downsizing is a change in the culture of the organization. That can be true for people as well.

Beyond the opportunity to scale back on expenses, some boomers we met moved as a deliberate strategy for escaping the bottleneck. The Hourglass Effect is a cumulative effect of decisions taken over decades: Moving house for whatever reason is likely to disturb old patterns and force you to rethink other aspects of your life as well.

Are You Working for Your Money, or Is Your Money Working for You?

The amount of money you have has, to some extent, defined your choices for decades: You worked to support a lifestyle for your family and yourself. Presumably you did that because it was satisfying. It is easy to forget that the lifestyle your money supports is subject to change—at will and at once. It is a choice like so many others—just another choice. Perhaps it is time to examine the choices you have made in the past and consider if they are still the ones you would like to make again, with the advantage of several decades of experience.

> **Paula:** Think about your lifestyle and what parts of your life are most satisfying now. If you were building your lifestyle from scratch, what would it look like? Would it be simpler or more complex?
>
> **Jeff:** Make a list of all your possessions. Now list them from most important to least important. If you were moving to another planet, which ones would you like to have with you?
>
> **Paula:** If you're like most of us, you haven't actually written down a budget in years. Do it now. You will probably be surprised at where your money goes each month—and how you might redirect it.

Jeff: You must change the way you think about money. That can be the greatest change agent of all. At the beginning of the chapter, we asked that you examine why you thought you didn't have enough money to make changes. The question isn't really how much money you need for retirement or change, the question is what you can do with the money you have.

What Can You Do with the Money You Have?

Almost anything. The essence of stuck is constraint. The essence of stuck is limitations. Sometimes, they are imposed by the circumstances of our lives, but very often, they are self-imposed. The difference between the people we met who were stuck in the hourglass and those who had emerged into Greater Adulthood had little to do with money. Those who were stuck at any income level were unable to take a fresh view of their situation and the amount of money accumulated. Or, they made the lack of money a ready excuse for inaction. Many were unwilling to consider even minor lifestyle adjustments that might enable them to leave a job they no longer enjoyed or a city they could no longer afford. We even met people who, for financial reasons, stayed with partners they no longer loved.

"We can't afford to get divorced."

Now, that's really stuck.

Money was not the controlling variable for most people as they created their Hourglass Solution. Thinking about money in a new way was. People who freed themselves from obligations, rents, jobs, and lifestyles that had grown constraining reaped benefits far beyond those that money can buy. Or, as it happens, it gave them what they had thought they couldn't afford: freedom.

Even though boomers may place a high value on personal freedom, they are no less vulnerable to the ties that bind middle-aged people to choices they made several decades earlier. The expectation of perpetual satisfaction has surely contributed to boomers' high divorce rate, high suicide rate, and conspicuous consumption, but the expectation can also be the impetus for productive self-analysis.

We live in a society and in a time in which materials goods are available on a truly impressive scale. But consumer goods alone will not be ultimately fulfilling to the boomer generation. In fact, the stress and pressures that often come with the ability to make unfettered purchases may not allow the purchaser to truly enjoy what was attained. Gregg Easterbrook has discussed this in *The Progress Paradox* and predicts that this clash of needs may be a decisive moment in our history: "A transition from material want to meaning want is in progress on an historically unprecedented scale—involving hundreds of millions of people—and may eventually be recognized as a principal cultural development of our age."[15]

> **Jeff:** Our consumption habits are just that—habits. There are choices to be made every day. It is a way to practice choice and control on a very personal level, and the impact of those choices is very immediate.
>
> **Paula:** An Hourglass Solution requires a broad-scale game change. Environmental issues,

economic climate, and reduced income for most boomers are all pointing in the same direction.

Jeff: Smart use of your own personal resources—energy, time, and money—will return maximum control.

Paula: Bingo, Einstein.

8

What If I Do Nothing?
Understanding Inertia

You will feel old. You will look old. You will hate your job. You will get fired. Or you will quit. The people in your life will bore you, and you will feel burdened by the responsibilities you used to handle easily. You might get divorced. No matter how much you saved or didn't save, you will be panicked about money. And someone close to you will become ill and need your help. None of this will feel good. This is the Hourglass Effect. The cumulative impact of decisions taken over several decades—all of them, the good ones and the unfortunate ones, the accidental triumphs and the deliberate catastrophes—have led us to this point.

You have reached a stage of life that needs to be addressed like all previous ones—childhood, adolescence, and young adulthood. Whether you stay stuck in the neck of the hourglass or break free and define new terrain for yourself is up to you. It is all about taking control of the reins of your life and making choices.

Stuck is a state of mind, and it is a very real place. It is a set of circumstances, and it is the inability to see that there are choices within any situation. Stuck can be a passage, or it can define the rest of your life.

In the preceding chapters, we have offered stories about boomers who are stuck in many different ways: stuck in their relationships, stuck in their work, stuck in patterns that aren't productive for them anymore. This chapter is about the urgency for change. It is about recognizing the many obstacles to creating your Hourglass Solution—and understanding them.

Matter that is in motion tends to stay in motion. Objects at rest stay still. The psychological pressure to justify and rationalize previous decisions can be overwhelming. We have heard and recounted dozens of stories of boomers who are stuck in the neck of the hourglass but apparently unable to make changes. They rationalize their current situations in ways that are unique to every person. But in the end, they are saying that the status quo is, at minimum, familiar and that new choices, by definition, are new and, by contrast, frightening.

Greater Adulthood begins with acknowledging that there is a problem. There is work to be done and changes to be made, and it may not be easy. Denial is the handmaiden of inertia. Most of us are deeply invested in the choices we have made to date. The road through young adulthood was costly on many dimensions: It required a vast outlay of emotional energy and hard work. There is enormous resistance to disturbing the delicate balance that has taken a lifetime to assemble, even when it's clear that your life is no longer really working.

> **Paula:** We want to stay in the house that we
> built with the people who are already assembled
> there and keep on smelling the roses we planted—

forever. We met many people who insisted that they loved their spouses and loved their work and felt no need to change anything at all.

Jeff: For a very few folks, that might turn out OK, but for most of us, doing nothing *is* the same as stuck, no matter how serene the water may appear. Doing nothing or changing nothing in midlife is almost always problematic.

Paula: The reality is, hardly anything stays the same. You change, the people around you change, your interests change—the world changes.

Jeff: It is an obvious point on a macro level—"yeah, sure, everything changes"—but most of us work very hard at "making things work" in our personal lives without making big changes. Much too scary.

Paula: But the truth is that Greater Adulthood is inaccessible without change. It doesn't happen automatically. Without an action plan, you are very likely to lose ground in all areas of your life—physically, emotionally, and vocationally.

Jeff: Access to Greater Adulthood will require effort and risk and the willingness to mess up your life a bit. But the consequence of inaction is likely to be far more debilitating.

Why You Must "Do Something" Now

The phenomenon of stuck is virtually universal. Stuck is as ubiquitous in midlife as sexual development is in adolescence. It goes with the territory. The difference between people is not in the occurrence of the disease, but in their willingness to define the cure.

Getting unstuck takes guts. For almost all the people we spoke with, it took a concerted effort to dismantle the life they had created—and reassemble their world in a new form. It took great courage, ruthless honesty, and dedicated energy. It takes courage to call out a problem when there is overwhelming pressure to ignore it. It takes ruthless honesty to begin a process of self-appraisal and not get mired in rationalization or blame or regret. And it takes great energy to overcome inertia.

The time to begin is now. Every day wasted is a day wasted. This is not a condition that gets resolved on its own. Deliberate and reasoned intervention is essential to maintain control and maximize options for the future.

The sense of powerlessness and loss of options is the most disabling side effect of aging. The absence of choice and the absence of control is a downward spiral from which there is rarely a return trip.

There is physical and psychological urgency to actively making choices and staying in control of your own life. Procrastination has never been a good technique; in midlife, it is dangerous. Postponing life choices is, for many boomers, a syndrome they have experienced at other times in their lives, with mixed results. For some, the decision to delay marriage, childbearing, and even a career has been helpful. Such deferrals allowed valuable maturing time before a person entered into long-term commitments. Changing attitudes about marriage and advances in fertility management have also freed us from some social and biological constraints. But for others, the delay of life decisions has been less productive. A generational insistence on rejecting some traditional age-related imperatives has left many boomers with fewer options than they anticipated. Midlife offers the opportunity not for do-over, but for real, personal growth. Postponement of this critical developmental phase is potentially hazardous.

> **Jeff:** Passive acceptance of the physical aspects of aging results in less and less energy. Boomers who act now have both the time and the strength to make significant life changes.
>
> **Paula:** The culture at large de-positions older adults. Without an aggressive plan, you are likely to become marginalized.
>
> **Jeff:** The cumulative impact of responsibilities that were taken on decades ago and new ones that may arrive with aging parents or grandkids can become a stranglehold without a strategy for managing them.
>
> **Paula:** And believe it or not, you are not going to live forever.

The psychological work of midlife is as important now as in any other life stage. When you were younger, you needed to become an autonomous person, separate and apart from your parents and family, and to develop a personal identity and capacity for intimacy with others.[1] Greater Adulthood continues the search for identity, but it is also about purpose and integrity. The bricks are work and relationships; the mortar is energy and money.

The psychological momentum to emerge from the neck of the hourglass comes from the effort of making sense of your life. This requires weaving the events into a coherent narrative that incorporates good decisions and bad ones, your own responsibilities and even the fickleness of fortune. When that work is done, you can move on and again make new choices without the past as a constant referent.

> **Paula:** New choices are not about reruns, repeats, or restitution. Many of us get caught up in trying to repeat our past successes—generally with diminishing returns—or even worse, redoing past failures but trying for a new and better outcome. This isn't a new choice; it is a compulsion.
>
> **Jeff:** The desire to repair damage and heal old wounds is common, but unlikely to happen by your simply trying again. The point is not to rewrite the story with a different ending, but to incorporate what has occurred and continue to develop the plot line of your life.
>
> **Paula:** The line between keeping up the good fight and futility is not always easy to determine—every virtue becomes a bore. Actually, every virtue becomes a whore.
>
> **Jeff:** Sometimes you are too smart for your own good.

Nostalgia and Regret: A Quagmire

The dual forces of nostalgia and regret have a seductive power to keep us locked in the neck of the hourglass. You can't recreate the past. You can't change the past. You can't undo the decisions you made years ago. And it isn't good for your health, either. Psychologists and physicians acknowledge the negative power of regret. Ruminating on paths not taken is a corrosive exercise creating heartaches and stomachaches as well. It rarely leads to positive action and, more often than not, is paralyzing. Nostalgia and regret are mainstays in the language of stuck:

> "I wanted to be an actor when I was younger. I had no support from my family, so it came to nothing. But I can't do anything about that now."

> "When I was married, we had an incredible house in Traverse City. Nothing I could buy now would even compare to that."

> "I had fifty people reporting to me. I'm not going to start doing my own typing at my age."

> "I really should have gone to art school. My husband was selfish. He didn't encourage me at all. But I'm too old for that now."

> "I just want one more chance to kick the can—to prove that I can do it—and that I still have what it takes."

Preoccupation with regret is insidious because it generally begins with a flabby assumption that if you had acted differently, or even worse, if *someone else* had acted differently, the outcome would have been better. It is a dangerous trap that rarely leads to positive action. Avoid future regret by moving forward with new plans rather than rerun the endless scenarios of what might have been. Being stuck in the past is a death sentence for the future.

> **Jeff:** Our advice: "Woulda-shoulda-coulda" is an isolating, nonproductive pastime.

Paula: Go to a movie if you feel regret coming on. Getting stalled at the start is a risk for those who don't have the courage to acknowledge their regrets and take responsibility for their life as it is.

Jeff: To some extent, we are all prisoners of our own intentions. We behave the same way, even in spite of evidence that the way we behave doesn't get us what we want. We change jobs—with the same outcome. We change partners—and change very little. The evidence is overwhelming: Without a deliberate program for changing behavior, we will simply repeat the same patterns.

Paula: By age fifty, the votes are in—you can see a pattern if you look for it. We tend to repeat the same mistakes and repeat what works as well.

Jeff: The opportunity is in deliberately sorting through the evidence and telling your story with integrity without getting caught up in particular traumas or successes or accidents.

Paula: Tell it with as much accuracy as possible—and that may take much revision. But when you get to something that approximates truth, you'll know it. Truth is the midwife who gets you out of the neck of the hourglass and into Greater Adulthood.

Regret isn't the only obstacle to moving forward. Some people have "choice amnesia"—they've simply forgotten how to make decisions. Some have "choice paralysis" because the consequences seem too overwhelming and the risks too great. Failure at something new seems more frightening than unhappiness with the status quo. Still others see themselves as passive players: Their past, present and future remains under the control of others.

Inertia can be exacerbated by social networks that depend on the tacit agreement of all participants for its solidarity. Common values, common behavior, and an agreed-upon pecking order are the glue that define community.

When an animal breaks away from the herd, the rest of the pack feels threatened. Like social animals everywhere, we expect to all travel in the same direction, doing the same thing, at the same time. And when we don't, it disrupts the equilibrium of the herd.

If our own mental roadblocks were not enough, we also discourage one another from achieving Greater Adulthood. All too often, the person making a life-changing decision is met with jealousy, anger, and even shock from friends and family. We may find that just when we need encouragement the most, our friends and family will, for their own reasons, need to withhold their support.

Ronald, now fifty-eight, described the transition time between the neck of the hourglass and his Hourglass Solution as a tunnel. "It's lonely in there," he told us. "It took about two years for Betty and me to make all the changes we wanted to make. There were all the usual complications and then some. It was hard going because we had all the fears about leaving our old life and none of the reinforcement of the new one we were constructing."

This can be a very vulnerable time. The best protection is to understand that the very people you hoped might help may be so threatened by your decision to step out and make changes that they simply cannot reach out to you.

Jeff: Our advice is to remember that you are the courageous one, and don't be disheartened. Much of the Hourglass Solution is like the transitions of youth—including the vulnerability to peer pressure. A great advantage in midlife is the wisdom to understand and resist it.

Paula: Any time a person departs from the norm, it threatens the solidarity of the group. In my ad-agency life, when someone quit, I generally asked the employee to leave right away and not stay the usual two weeks, because his or her continued presence was threatening to the others. Unconsciously, it made all the employees reconsider their own choices.

When Edna made the life-changing decision to quit her job and move to another state, she received a few notes of congratulations, but most were expressions of shock and bewilderment: "I don't know why I cried when I heard the news," wrote one coworker. "Well, [I] welled up. But I did and am welled up now. Change. What a strange thing. How young and vibrant to engage in it. Wow! I just hope you know what you're doing. Must go and will write later."

The writer relegates change to the young and seems to reject the possibility of change in later years. And there is an underlying tone of jealousy and a wagging finger: "I hope you know what you're doing."

A successful Hourglass Solution is not about making the perfect choice. There is no single right choice. The Hourglass Solution is about increasing options and possibilities in later life. It's about asking yourself, is the decision I am about to make going to increase my options for the future or decrease them? Will it expand my horizons or confine them? What-if scenarios that consistently focus on negative outcomes are just another manifestation of stuck.

Postponements and delays are sometimes prudent. If they result in greater information or greater resources, then we can safely call it "planning." But some decisions are time-limited.

> **Paula:** Recently, we met a man in an elevator. He was tan and fit and appeared to be in his early sixties. He explained that he had just returned from a three-year sailing adventure around the world.
>
> **Jeff:** We were thrilled to meet him. Like so many of the people we interviewed for this book, he had calculated what he could do– and he took the leap.
>
> **Paula:** We complimented him on his courage and told him that we were also contemplating making some major changes in our lives. Sizing us up and, presumably, guessing our ages, he advised us: "If you're going to have a personal renaissance, do it now. Because once you've turned sixty, you're going to be too tired, too comfortable, or too something. Because stuff happens at that age. If you're going to do it, do it now."
>
> **Jeff:** He went on to tell us about his friend, a pediatrician, with whom he had shared the sail-away fantasy for years. The pediatrician found many reasons not to go—work, family, money, time. So our friend left on his own, with his dog as his only companion.

Paula: Now, three years later, the pediatrician has developed a chronic illness and will never make that trip.

Jeff: Carpe diem.

9

Greater Adulthood: All Aboard

This train is leaving the station. The certain truth is that a year from now, you will be one year older, or you will be dead. It is time to embark on the journey to Greater Adulthood—a journey that will define the rest of your life.

Where We Are Now

The first decades of boomer adulthood have seen unprecedented change and achievements. We grew up. We have assumed power positions in government, industry, science, and the arts. There has been much good news. Great strides have been made in achieving equal rights for all Americans. Despite the downturn of 2008, the economy has grown through innovation and invention—an American habit that boomers have put their own distinctive stamp on. We have become polymorphic communicators, facile in media that were invented for us and by us.

We have become a planet. The awareness of a global universe and our responsibility for it has come in fits and starts, but at minimum, our generation has acknowledged that we are not in this alone. We have cloned sheep and achieved medical breakthroughs that have delivered twins to the childless, arrested AIDS for the fortunate, controlled cancers, and repaired, transplanted, or built vital organs.

We had eighty million children and sent more of them to college than did any other generation. We worked hard, growing the gross domestic product from $1.7 trillion in 1950 to $11.7 trillion in 2008 and made the eighty-hour workweek a common occurrence.[1]

Although boomers during this period of sustained effort have been highly productive and are proud of their accomplishments, midlife demands a course correction. Responsibilities and obligations, commitments and promises—most willingly undertaken with all the restrictions and satisfactions that accompanied them—are no longer providing the sense of fulfillment and personal happiness we have come to expect. This is the neck of the hourglass.

The question for baby boomers is whether the generation that has been the pacesetter in the political, social, and economic life of the nation will continue to be change agents in later life. Will they be the ill-fated inheritors of the hourglass, stuck with a longer life span than ever imagined but holding a set of consequences that are antithetical to every life-affirming instinct they have experienced to date? Will the generation that redefined every major life stage it has passed through stop at age fifty?

Paula: Hell no!

Jeff: There is every reason to be hopeful. And we are. Boomers are the most numerous and most diverse generation in history. But if there was an overarching attitude that describes this generation, we would choose *optimism*.

Paula. Paradoxically, even the boomers who understand they are stuck can have positive expectations for the future. Cheerfully shrugging off their lack of savings, dire predictions about social security, and the implications of an overpriced and underdelivered care system, two-thirds of us said in a recent study that we felt good about the future.[2]

Jeff: The instinct for happiness is very strong in baby boomers—we are not a generation of fatalists. We have energy and inclination. The effort and creativity required to break free and to again experience the breadth of choices that will provide control and fulfillment for the rest of our lives has been the subject of this book. The promise and opportunity are ripe for harvest.

Paula: The journey begins and ends with you. You will need to decide what you can do. Stay in the job you have, or start a new career. Stay in the house you've lived in for years, or move to a different neighborhood, another city, or even a foreign country. You will need to decide what you can do with the money you have—not just what you *can't* do. And you will need to decide whether your family and friends are helping or hurting your chance for personal fulfillment.

Jeff: This process of focusing on one's own dreams and aspirations is a bit of an archeological dig for some. So many of the people we spoke to found it almost impossible to answer the question "What do *you* want to do?" Invariably, their responses were buried under mountains of interconnected responsibilities and commitments.

Paula: At midlife you are not a clean slate, but the Hourglass Solution asks that you imagine yourself without the constraints that other people and long-standing commitments bring. Just set them aside like a jacket or a heavy pair of boots— you can pick them up later if you still want them.

Jeff: The irony is that boomers, so often criticized for their narcissism, have become more like their parents than anyone would have expected— shouldering all the responsibilities of adulthood and then some. But our continued expectations of perpetual happiness and new experience and our refusal to accept what were the traditional inevitabilities of age have created a different set of imperatives.

Paula: Greater Adulthood beckons.

What You Need for the Journey

Some people have had wonderful success in breaking free from the neck of the hourglass and redefining the landscape of their lives. Some are irrevocably stuck. The fault line appears to be about character and courage. Character often eludes description, but we know it when we see it—a pesky streak of honesty; a tendency to see the situation as it really is; and a proclivity to do the hard, right thing versus the easy, wrong one. Our role models for seeking the Hourglass Solution seem to have it. In fact, we all have it—we only need to find it beneath the layers of denial and accommodation.

Character will keep you honest, but courage is the most important attribute in developing your Hourglass Solution. Courage doesn't mean that you are not afraid. On the contrary, all change carries with it a degree of risk, and with risk comes the possibility of error. But courage is the part of character that allows you to keep your goal in mind and persist, even when the outcome is unclear or the support for your efforts is not forthcoming. Courage gets you out of the neck of the hourglass to the best adventure of your life. Character is what enables you to identify that you are stuck—but it is courage that will see you through.

Courage provides us with choices. It deflects us from the single track of inevitable consequence. The wail of "I have no choice" has no place in a courageous life, because even in the worst of situations, there are options. The difference between a courageous person and one who is not is in the willingness to choose rather than accept consequences. There will always be the unexpected outcome, the disappointing result, or the unattainable goal, but we will rarely experience bitterness if we have acted deliberately. Character enables courage, and this will make all the difference.

After many decades of a life marked by responsibilities—often joyfully assumed and then conscientiously pursued—it is sometimes hard to find the courage to step away from them. The culture is reluctant to grant this opportunity, and our years "in service" to those responsibilities make the constraints feel normal and even comfortable. Permission to think and act differently is inevitably self-determined.

For many, their Hourglass Solution came together simply when they left the emotional space for a transformation to occur. It is hard to find answers or even see alternatives that are right in front of us if we remain committed to the patterns of a lifetime. By the time we are in our forties and fifties, our daily schedules are unlikely to contain much slack time. In fact, we get to like it that way. We measure our success by our productivity—how much you can "get done" in a single day. By midlife, most of us have gotten quite expert at squeezing in nearly every activity we have determined is important, plus some. Work, family, community, exercise, friends, and hobbies—even the laziest among us have "calendars." In fact, the thought of a day without entries—without the familiarity of a well-traveled routine—is often unsettling. Free time isn't free; it's anxiety producing. So, we manage it by never having any. We don't leave spaces, not in our days and, inevitably, not in our heads.

> **Jeff:** We found that most people who have successfully emerged from the hourglass did so over time. The process was ongoing—often for many years. The realization that they were stuck took time. We all say, "Everything is fine" for as long as we can get away with it.
>
> **Paula:** Until we realize that we feel hopeless and that there appears to be no way out. Stuck. The journey out of the bottleneck takes time. There needs to be some mental space to travel from the land of "I should" to the place where "I want." It takes time and space to realize that you can dramatically change your life.

Jeff: We often tell young people to take it easy and not to rush major life decisions. We encourage college kids to take a gap year during or after school because we believe that time away will help them make better choices.

Paula: The prerequisites of time and space for making choices and changes are essentially the same for us in midlife.

Jeff: That realization begins the process of self-discovery and renewal. Here is where the exciting work begins. And it necessarily begins with you. When you can begin to imagine the breadth of possibility that you can gain access to and how much better you will feel, you are on your way.

The Promise of Greater Adulthood

The specific coordinates of Greater Adulthood will be different for everyone. Full realization of the Hourglass Solution means making a life of one's own exclusive design. The stories in this book are meant to suggest the possibilities that are available, but there are innumerable permutations and combinations yet to be invented. The Hourglass Solution will be different for everyone, but the unifying vision is a fully authentic life, a life of your own choosing. In an authentic life, we do the things we choose to do, understanding that there are options. We choose control over consequence, honesty over artifice. The choices you make may not always be pleasant, but they will always serve a goal you have actively embraced. You will inevitably respond—and fulfill—the needs of others, but always as an expression of your authentic self. You will make choices—not sacrifices.

> **Paula:** The distinction between choice and sacrifice is all the difference in the world. Although sometimes it seems as if there are no good choices, the act of choosing grants you control—even in bad situations.
>
> **Jeff:** Choosing a course of action, as opposed to succumbing to outside demands, is what gives life authenticity and makes behavior genuine.
>
> **Paula:** It's not always possible to understand why we do what we do—we do hide from ourselves. But authentic choices, made from an understanding of who you are as a person—not who you were, not who someone else wants you to be—are inevitably easier to live with.
>
> **Jeff:** We can't always control the circumstance of our lives, but we can control how we respond to them. And that is a critical difference.

The promise of Greater Adulthood is a life with the vitality of youth seasoned by the experience of a lifetime. The joy of it is the excitement and anticipation of fresh experience. It is an energy-recovery program. Habits of a lifetime create robotic behavior. The same physical activity repeated over time uses less and less energy—the body accommodates. People who are going through the motion of relationships or the daily activities of life acquire a kind of vagueness that is recognizable at a glance. The exuberance of youthful energy is again available with the exercise of choice.

Paula: We can't guarantee that you will be leaping tall buildings in a single bound. But people who are free of the constraints of an outgrown life do seem to have a spring in their step.

Jeff: Stress in midlife is often about conflict—the conflict between doing what you choose and doing what you think you have to do. That creates resentment and bitterness, and it will suck you dry.

Paula: Energy is the fountain of youth in Greater Adulthood. I know a guy who is in the midst of creating his Hourglass Solution. He is in transition, and some parts are messy—a pending divorce, adult kids who still need help, a house for sale in a bad market—but every time I see him, he looks younger and more vivid. I once saw a picture of him when he was about thirteen or fourteen: a beautiful kid with a smile that said he just knew life was going to be grand. And last week when I saw him, he had that smile again.

The Road Ahead: Ready for Anything

What will it feel like when we are through the neck of the hourglass? That's like asking what it will feel like when you fall in love. It will be different for everyone, because you will feel like you, only better than you have felt in years. The promise of the Hourglass Solution is authenticity of action in every aspect of your life, from your intimate relationships to the most casual encounters. You will give and receive love and friendship in a more honest and genuine way than you may have experienced in a long time, because you will chose the people you want to be with. Most of them may be the same—or they might be very different. You might live in a different place that gives your identity a real lift. You may find new work that allows you to use your skills in a new way and create value of a different kind. Or perhaps you will develop a talent or interest that you've had neither the time nor the inclination to nurture. You will feel nervous and excited, eager and energetic. The world will seem like an exciting place. The work of coming through the neck of the hourglass is a process of stripping down. The goal is to emerge lighter and more buoyant.

> **Jeff:** Travel light with as little baggage as possible—that will provide maximum maneuverability in this new life stage. Take *who* you love and *what* you love. But if you shed the unnecessary weight, you will be flexible enough to truly consider new options.
>
> **Paula:** No one can tell you that every day will be a holiday on the other side of the bottleneck. Life will always be complicated with good times and bad ones. You will experience the full range of emotions—maybe you haven't done that for a while. That's why it takes courage. Sitting on the back porch doesn't take much at all.
>
> **Jeff:** And that is the whole point. Stuck in the neck of the hourglass, we experience a grinding sameness—with diminishing returns. The alternative of Greater Adulthood is the recovery of adventure, risk, and reward. Not everything that happens there will be wonderful. But we think you

will be glad you came. Understanding that there are choices in everything that we do is nothing short of liberating. The Hourglass Solution is about making new choices and taking control of the rest of your life.

Paula: It doesn't get better than that.

Notes

Chapter 1
The Hourglass Effect: A Boomer Epidemic

1. As quoted by Abigail Trafford, *My Time* (New York: Basic Books, 2004).

2. Deborah S. Hasin et al., "Epidemiology of Major Depressive Dis orders," *Archives of General Psychiatry* 62, no. 10 (October 2005): 1097–1106.

3. "Depression Risk 'Highest in 40s,'" *BBC News America*, January 29, 2008, http://bbc.co.uk/1/hi/health/7213387.stm.

4. U.S. Department of Health and Human Services, Substance Abuse and Mental Health Services Administration, Results from the *2006 National Survey on Drug Use and Health: National Findings*, NSDUH Series H-32, DHHS Publication No. SMA 07–4293 (Rockville, MD: SAMHSA, Office of Applied Studies, 2007), http://oas.samhsa.gov/nsduh/2k6nsduh/2k6Results.pdf.

5. Lee Bowman, Lisa Hoffman, and Thomas Hargrove, "Boomer Doom: Falling Victim to the Culture of Youth," *Scripps News*, January 24, 2007.

6. Tucker Sutherland, "Senior Citizens at Highest Risk of Dying from Suicide and about Anything Else, Actually," *Senior Journal*, September 19, 2007, www.seniorjournal.com/NEWS/Features/2007/7-09-19-SenCitAtHighestRisk.htm.

7. As quoted by Bowman, Hoffman, and Hargrove, "Boomer Doom."

8. The MIDUS survey was administered to a national sample of 7,189 U.S. adults aged twenty-five to seventy-four. It was the first research to

include epidemiological, sociological, and psychological measures in a single study. Results reported by Orville Gilbert Brin, Carol D. Ryff, and Ronald C. Kessler, eds., *How Healthy Are We? A National Study of Well-Being at Midlife* (Chicago: University of Chicago Press, 2004).

9. Ute Kunzmann, "Perceiving Control: A Double-Edged Sword in Old Age," *Journals of Gerontology Series B*, Psychological Sciences & Social Sciences 57B, no. 6 (2002): 484–491; Margie E. Lachman and Kimberly M. Prenda Firth, "The Adaptive Value of Feeling in Control during Midlife," in *How Healthy Are We? A National Study of Well-Being at Midlife*, ed. Orville Gilbert Brin, Carol D. Ryff, and Ronald C. Kessler (Chicago: University of Chicago Press, 2004), 320–349; Hazel Rose Markus, Victoria C. Plant, and Margie E. Lachman, "Well-Being in America: Core Features and Regional Patterns," in *How Healthy Are We? A National Study of Well-Being at Midlife*, ed. Orville Gilbert Brin, Carol D. Ryff, and Ronald C. Kessler (Chicago: University of Chicago Press, 2004), 614–650.

Chapter 2
Boomerology: The Generational Experience

1. Figure for percentage of baby boomer men serving in Vietnam based on statistics from the U.S. Department of Defense and reported in *Mobile Riverine Force Association*, "Vietnam War Statistics," www.mrfa.org/vnstats.htm.

2. Based on U.S. Department of Defense statistics and reported in ibid.

3. The military draft lottery began in 1970 and assigned priority draft numbers on the basis of the individual's birthday—men with low numbers were drafted first.

4. U.S. Census Bureau, *Decennial Census of Population, 1940 to 2000*, www.census.gov/prod/cen2000/doc/sf3.pdf.

5. The American Society for Aesthetic Plastic Surgery, *Cosmetic Surgery National Data Bank 2006 Statistics* (New York: ASAPA Communications Office, 2007), www.surgery.org/download/2006stats.pdf.

6. For incidence of hip and other joint-replacement surgeries, see T. Dixon, M. Shaw, S. Ebrahim, and P. Dieppe, "Trends in Hip and New Joint Replacement: Socioeconomic Inequalities and Projections of Need," *Annals of the Rheumatic Diseases* 63, no. 7 (July 2004): 825–830. For numbers on artificial organs and transplants, see P. M. Galletti, "Organ Replacement: Basic Research and Perspective," paper presented at

International Society of Technology Assessment in Health Care meeting, 1993, http://gateway.nlm.nih.gov/MeetingAbstracts/ma?f=102211411 .html.

7. From the U.S. Census Bureau, *The 2008 Statistical Abstract, The National Data Book*, and reported by Claritas, Inc., www.claritas.com/ samples/sitereports/hh_income_by_age_of_householder_06.pdf.

8. Home ownership data reported by the U.S. Census, *Housing Vacancies and Home Ownership*, CPS/HVS, www.census.gov/hhes/ www/housing/hvs/qtr208/q208ind.html.

9. U.S. Department of Labor, Bureau of Labor Statistics, *Issues in Labor Statistics: Spending Patterns by Age*, August 2000, www.bls.gov/ opub/ils/pdf/opbils41.pdf.

10. U.S. Department of Labor, Bureau of Labor Statistics, *Consumer Expenditures in 2005*, February 2007, www.bls.gov/cex/csxann05.pdf.

11. Martin E. P. Seligman, *Learned Optimism: How to Change Your Mind and Your Life* (New York: Vintage Books, 2006).

12. Darrin M. McMahon, *Happiness: A History* (New York: Atlantic Monthly Press, 2006).

13. Abraham Maslow based his theory on a hypothetical hierarchy of needs. The most basic needs are physiological, followed by needs for safety and security. Once those have been satisfied, the person can move up the ladder to love, belonging, and self-esteem. Only if all those needs have been met can the individual become self-actualized. For further information on Maslow's theories, see Abraham H. Maslow, *Toward a Psychology of Being* (New York: J. Wiley & Sons, 1999).

Chapter 3
Stuck in the Hourglass: The Straitjacket of Midlife

1. Deborah F. Tannen is a professor of linguistics at Georgetown University in Washington, DC, and has authored numerous books on the subject of interpersonal communication, including *That's Not What I Meant! How Conversational Style Makes or Breaks Relationships* (New York: Ballantine, 1986); and *You Just Don't Understand: Women and Men in Conversation* (New York: William Morrow, 1990).

2. For additional information about the stages of life, see Erik H. Erikson, *Identity and the Life Cycle* (New York: W.W. Norton, 1980); and Erik H. Erikson, Joan M. Erikson, and Helen Q. Kivnick, *Vital Involvement in Old Age* (New York: W. W. Norton, 1986).

Chapter 4
The People in Our Lives: Renovating Relationships

1. Household composition combinations included all permutations of extended and blended families as well as nonfamily members residing in a family dwelling unit. Reported by Frank Hobbs, U.S. Census Bureau, *Examining American Household Composition: 1990 and 2000*, Census 2000 special report CENSR-24 (Washington, DC: U.S. Government Printing Office, 2005), www.census.gov/prod/2005pubs/censr-24.pdf.

2. Data gathered from Segal Company, "The Aging of Aquarius: The Baby Boom Generation Matures," *Segal Special Report*, Segal Company, New York, February 2001, www.segalco.com/publications/segalspecial reports/feb01aquarius.pdf.

3. U.S. Census Bureau, *Census 2000 Brief: Marital Status*, October 2003, www.census.gov/prod/2003pubs/c2kbr-30.pdf; and U.S. Census Bureau, *Census 2000 Special Reports: Married-Couple and Unmarried-Partner Households 2000*, February 2003, www.census.gov/prod/2003pubs/censr-5.pdf.

4. David Popenoe, "The State of Our Unions: The Social Health of Marriage in America, 2007," National Marriage Project at Rutgers University, Piscataway, NJ, 2007.

5. U.S. Census Bureau, *Census 2000 Brief: Marital Status*; and James E. Thomas, Jr., "Statistics" page on "The Widow's Bridge" Web site, www.widowsbridge.com/stats.asp.

6. U.S. Department of Health and Human Services, Administration on Aging, *A Profile of Older Americans: 2004*, www.aoa.gov/PROF/Statistics/profile/2004/9.aspx.

7. Nadine F. Marks, Larry L. Bumpass, and Heyjung Jun, "Family Roles and Well-Being During the Middle Life Course," in *How Healthy Are We? A National Study of Well-Being at Midlife*, ed. Orville Gilbert Brin, Carol D. Ryff, and Ronald C. Kessler (Chicago: University of Chicago Press, 2004), 514–549.

8. Trend-analysis organization Iconoculture found that families with aging parents spend an average of 10 percent of their income to care for their parents (Molly Priesmeyer, "Caring for Aging Parents Is Taking a Toll on U.S. Families," Iconoculture Report, December 14, 2007, www.iconoculture.com/Article/Observation.aspx?DocName=oa_Caregi vingfortheelde_91319).

9. Blanche Evans, "New Studies from Del Webb Show Kids Boomerang on Boomers," *Realty Times*, July 6, 2004, http://realtytimes .com/rtpages/20040706_boomerang.htm.

10. U.S. Census Bureau, "An Older and More Diverse Population by Mid-Century," *U.S. Census Bureau News,* press release, August 14, 2008.

Chapter 5
Getting Energy Back: Reengaging with the World

1. Comila Shahani-Denning, R. L. Dipboye, and T. M. Gehrlein, "Attractiveness Bias in the Interview: Exploring the Boundaries of an Effect," *Basic and Applied Social Psychology* 14 (1993): 317–328.

2. Charla Krupp, *How Not to Look Old: Fast and Effortless Ways to Look 10 Years Younger, 10 Pounds Lighter, 10 Times Better* (New York: Springboard Press, 2008).

3. Vonda Wright with Ruth Winter, *Fitness After 40: How to Stay Strong at Any Age* (New York: AMACOM, 2008).

4. Robert Langreth, "Want to Live Forever?" *Forbes*, November 14, 2005.

5. Peter Keating, "Why Do the Elderly Dress So Badly? No, Really," SmartMoney.com, July 25, 2007, www.smartmoney.com/thenew retirement/index.cfm?story=august2007.

6. Kathleen Fackelmann, "Belly Fat Linked to an Increased Risk of Dementia," *USA Today*, March 27, 2008.

7. Beth J. Soldo et al., "Cross-Cohort Differences in Health on the Verge of Retirement," working paper 12762, National Bureau of Economic Research, Cambridge, MA, December 2006.

8. Miranda Hitti, "Baby Boomers in Bad Shape: Study Shows Boomers in Poorer Health than Pre-World War II Group at Same Age," WebMD.com, March 6, 2007, www.webmd.com/healthy-aging/news/20070306/baby-boomers-in-bad-shape.

9. *Advertising Age*, Data Center 1992–2008, "Domestic Ad Spending by Category," http://adage.com/datacenter/datapopup.php?article_id =118673; and *Advertising Age*, Data Center 1992–2008, "U.S. Company Revenue per 2006 Ad Dollar," http://adage.com/datacenter/datapopup.php?article_id=118677.

10. American Society for Aesthetic Plastic Surgery, *Cosmetic Surgery National Data Bank 2006 Statistics* (New York: ASAPA Communications Office, 2007), www.surgery.org/download/2006stats.pdf.

11. Study conducted by Medco Health Solutions, Inc., and reported by the Associated Press, "Americans Taking Prescription Drugs in Greater Numbers," *New York Times*, May 14, 2008.

12. Linda Bren, "Joint Replacement: An Inside Look," U.S. Food and Drug Administration *FDA Consumer Magazine*, March–April 2004, Pub No. FDA 04–1335C, www.fda.gov/fdac/features/2004/204_joints.html.

13. Denise Mann, "Joint Replacement Surgery on the Rise," *WebMD Health News*, March 24, 2006, www.medscape.com/viewarticle/528464.

14. Tara Parker-Pope, "Reinventing Date Night for Long-Married Couples," *New York Times*, February 12, 2008.

15. Gene D. Cohen, *The Mature Mind: The Positive Power of the Aging Brain* (New York: Basic Books, 2005).

16. U.S. Department of Health and Human Services, National Institute on Aging, "Alzheimer's Disease Fact Sheet," July 24, 2008, www.nia.nih.gov/alzheimers/publications/adfact.htm.

17. Sara Reistad-Long, "Older Brain Really May Be a Wiser Brain," *New York Times*, May 20, 2008.

18. Becca Levy, "Improving Memory in Old Age through Implicit Self-Stereotyping," *Journal of Personality and Social Psychology* 71 (1996): 1092–1107.

19. U.S. Department of Education, Office of Vocational and Adult Education, "Adult Education Facts at a Glance," September 20, 2002, www.ed.gov/about/offices/list/ovae/pi/AdultEd/aefacts.html.

20. N. Susan Emeagwali, "Community Colleges Offer Baby Boomers an Encore," *Techniques: Connecting Education and Careers* (publication of the Association for Career and Technical Education), October 2007, www.acteonline.org/members/techniques/2006–2007/upload/Thm1.pdf.

21. Alvaro Fernandez, "Brain Health Research Business Grows with Research and Demand," *Aging Today* (publication of American Society on Aging), March–April 2008.

22. Jin Bongguk, "Social Psychological Determinants of Life Satisfaction in Older Adults," Ph.D. dissertation, Indiana University, Bloomington, August 2001, *Dissertation Abstracts International Section A: Humanities & Social Sciences* 62, no. 2-A: 769.

23. Raksha Arora and James Harter, "Nearly As Many Americans Struggling as Thriving," Gallup.com Web site, April 29, 2008, www.gallup.com/poll/106906/Nearly-Many-Americans-Struggling-Thriving.aspx.

24. Pew Research Center, "From the Age of Aquarius to the Age of Responsibility: Baby Boomers Approach Age 60," December 8, 2005, http://pewresearch.org/assets/social/pdf/socialtrends-boomers120805.pdf.

25. Corinne Asturias, "Stayin' Alive: Survivorship Becomes Paradigm Shift for People Facing Disease," Iconoculture Report, December 3, 2004, www.iconoculture.com/Article/Trend.aspx?DocName=ta_Survivorship _38331.

26. Po Bronson, *What Should I Do with My Life?* (New York: Random House, 2003).

27. George A. Bonanno, "Loss, Trauma, and Human Resilience: Have We Underestimated the Human Capacity to Thrive after Extremely Aversive Events?" *American Psychologist* 59 (March 2005): 20–28.

28. Carolyn M. Aldwin, Avron Spiro III, and Crystal L. Park, "Health Behavior and Optimal Aging: A Life Span Developmental Perspective," in *Handbook of the Psychology of Aging*, ed. James E. Birren and K. Warner Schaie (Burlington, MA: Elsevier Academic Press, 2006).

29. Anne Underwood, "For a Happy Heart: Depression, Loneliness, and Anger Take a Toll on Cardiac Health; New Research Shows How to Help," *Newsweek International*, October 4, 2004.

Chapter 6
Our Work: Risk, Renewal, and Retirement

1. Department for Professional Employees, AFL-CIO, *Current Statistics on White Collar Employees* (Washington, DC: Department for Professional Employees, AFL-CIO, 2003), www.dpeaflcio.org/pdf/2003 _GeneralChartbook(ALL).pdf.

2. Job-change data from U.S. Bureau of Labor Statistics, "Number of Jobs Held, Labor Market Activity, and Earnings Growth among the Youngest Baby Boomers: Results from a Longitudinal Survey," July 27, 2008, www.bls.gov/news.release/nlsoy.nr0.htm; layoff statistics from Richard W. Johnson, Gordon B. T. Mermin, and Matthew Resseger, "Employment at Older Ages and the Changing Nature of Work," AARP Public Policy Institute Report (Washington, DC: AARP, November 2007).

3. AARP, "Update on the Aged 55+ Worked: 2005," *Data Digest* 136 (April 2006).

4. Hans Eisenbeis, "Old Enough to Know Better: Entrepreneurial Spirit Growing Among Boomers and Matures," Iconoculture Report, January 29, 2008, www.iconoculture.com/Article/Trend.aspx?DocName =ta_BoomerSelfEmployment_92618.

5. Philip Janson and Jack K. Martin, "Job Satisfaction and Age: A Test of Two Views," *Social Forces* 60, no. 4 (June 1982): 1089–1102.

6. Lynn Franco, "Job Satisfaction Continues to Whither," Conference Board executive action report A-0069–03-EA, September 2003, www.conference-board.org/cgi-bin/MsmGo.exe?grab_id=0& EXTRA_ARG=&SCOPE=Public&host_id=42&page_id=2343&query =job%20satisfaction&hiword=satisfaction%20SATISFACTORY%20 job%20.

7. Louis Uchitelle, *The Disposable American: Layoffs and Their Consequences* (New York: Vintage Books, 2007).

8. Alan M. Webber, "Beware of Angry, Jobless Men," *USA Today*, September 8, 2003.

9. John Helyar, "Fifty and Fired," *Fortune*, May 16, 2005.

10. AARP, "Update."

11. Lynn A. Karoly and Julie Zissimopoulos, "Self-Employment Among Older U.S. Workers," *Monthly Labor Review* 127 no. 7 (July 2004): 24–47, www.bls.gov/opub/mlr/2004/07/lmir.htm.

12. Carolyn A. Martin and Bruce Tulgan, *Managing the Generation: from Urgency to Opportunity* (Amherst, MA: HRD Press, 2006).

13. As quoted by Helyar, "Fifty and Fired."

14. U.S. Bureau of Labor Statistics, "Displaced Workers Earnings at New Job: January 2008," (August 27, 2008), http://www.bls.gov/opub/ ted/2008/aug/wk4/art03.htm.

15. AARP, "Update."

16. Sara Davidson, *Leap! What Will We Do with the Rest of Our Lives?* (New York: Ballantine Books, 2008).

17. S. Kathi Brown, *Staying Ahead of the Curve 2003: The AARP Working in Retirement Study* (Washington, DC: AARP Knowledge Management, 2003).

18. Williams Graebner, *History of Retirement: The Meaning and Function of an American Institution, 1885–1978* (New Haven: Yale University Press, 1980).

19. American Institute of Certified Public Accountants, *Understanding Social Security Reform: The Issues and Alternatives*, 2nd ed. (New York: American Institute of Certified Public Accountants, March 2005).

20. Barbara A. Butrica, Eric J. Toder, and Desmond J. Toohey, *Boomers at the Bottom: How Will Low-Income Boomers Cope with Retirement* (Washington, DC: AARP Public Policy Institute, March 2008).

21. Teresa T. King and H. Wayne Cecil, "The History of Major Changes to the Social Security System," *CPA Journal* (published by the

New York State Society of CPAs), May 2006, www.nysscpa.org/
cpajournal/2006/506/infocus/p15.htm.

22. Corporation for National and Community Service, "Volunteer
Growth in America: A Review of Trends since 1974," *Volunteering in
America*, November 2006, www.nationalservice.gov/pdf/06_1203
_volunteer_growth.pdf.

23. Corporation for National and Community Service, "Keeping
Baby Boomers Volunteering: A Research Brief on Volunteer Retention
and Turnover," March 2007, www.nationalservice.gov/pdf/07_0307
_boomer_report.pdf.

24. Suzanne Perry and Michael Aft, "Make Room for Boomers,"
Chronicle of Philanthropy 18, no. 4 (November 24, 2005): 6–14.

Chapter 7
Our Money: Rethinking Dollars and Sense

1. Tim Westrich, "Problems with Plastic: Credit Card Debt Hits
Record High," Center for American Progress, April 18, 2008,
www.americanprogress.org/issues/2008/04/plastic_problems.html.

2. Christian E. Weller, "Drowning in Debt," report, Center for
American Progress, Washington, D.C., May 11, 2006.

3. Jane Birnbaum, "An Alternative to Annuities for Retirees Seeking
Income," *New York Times*, November 11, 2007, C3.

4. Daniel Kadlec, "Everyone Back in the Labor Pool: Eroding Pension
Benefits, Longer Life-Spans and a Major Meltdown in Stocks Add Up to
This: Most of Us Will Have to Work Well into Our 70s," *Time*, July 29,
2002, 22ff.

5. For changes in household size, see "This New House," *Mother
Jones*, March–April 2005.

6. Molly Priesmeyer, "Meet the New Debt Addicts," *Iconoculture Report*, March 18, 2008.

7. Elizabeth Warren and Amelia Warren Tyagi, *The Two-Income Trap:
Why Middle-Class Mothers and Fathers Are Going Broke* (New York: Basic
Books, 2003).

8. U.S. Bureau of Labor Statistics, "Consumer Expenditures in
2005," report 998, February 2007, www.bls.gov/cex/csxann05.pdf.

9. Leslie M. Harris and Michelle Edelman, *After Sixty: Marketing to
Baby Boomers Reaching Their Big Transition Years* (Ithaca, NY: Paramount
Marketing Publishing, 2006).

10. U.S. Bureau of Labor Statistics, "Consumer Expenditure Survey 2006," www.bls.gov/cex/2006/Standard/age.pdf.

11. David Brooks, "The Great Seduction," *New York Times*, June 10, 2008.

12. Abby Duly, "Consumer Spending on Necessities," *Consumer Expenditure Survey Anthology* (2003): 35–38, www.bls.gov/cex/anthology/csxanth6.pdf.

13. "Un-necessities: Americans Spend a Lot on Things They Don't Need," Iconoculture Report, November 22, 2002.

14. Martin John Brown, "Too Much Stuff! America's New Love Affair with Self-Storage," *AlterNet*, June 4, 2008, www.alternet.org/workplace/86998/.

15. Gregg Easterbrook, *The Progress Paradox* (New York: Random House, 2003).

Chapter 8
What If I Do Nothing? Understanding Inertia

1. For more information on life stage development, see Erik Erikson, *Identity and the Life Cycle* (New York: W.W. Norton, 1980; reissued 1994); and Erik Erikson, *The Life Cycle Completed: A Review* (New York: W.W. Norton, 1982).

Chapter 9
Greater Adulthood: All Aboard

1. The gross domestic product figure is from U.S. Department of Commerce Bureau of Economic Analysis, Gross Domestic Product, as measured in 2000 dollars, http://research.stlouisfed.org/fred2/data/GDPC1.txt.

2. Lydia Saad, "An Inexplicable Jump in Americans' Long-Term Optimism: Two-Thirds Expect Conditions in the U.S. Five Years from Now to Be Positive," Gallup Poll, January 23, 2008, www.gallup.com/poll/103873/Inexplicable-Jump-Americans-LongTerm-Optimism.aspx.

Acknowledgments

We thank Matthew Lore for taking a chance on us and for his ruthlessly honest assessment of the original manuscript. Matthew made us write a better book.

We also are most grateful to all our fellow boomers who shared their stories with us. These stories were exciting and troubling, revealing and inspiring. They defined the Hourglass Effect and, ultimately, the Hourglass Solution.

This book had many midwives: friends and relatives who assured us that the idea was an important one and that it was worth the considerable sacrifice required to bring it to completion. Thanks to all—especially Arlene Bouras, Izzy Forman, and Lukas Volger.

Last, we acknowledge the power of partnership. Two heads are better than one—and ever so much more fun.

About the Authors

Jeff Johnson, PhD, has had multiple careers and expects to have several more. He has worked as a psychologist for the New York State Office for the Aging and the New York City Department for the Aging. He has taught graduate school and has worked at some of the most prestigious ad agencies in the country, including his current role as general manager of independent ad agency, Cramer Krasselt. Along with Paula, Jeff founded Hourglass, Inc., a consulting company designed to help other boomers find their own Hourglass Solutions.

Paula Forman had a long and distinguished career in the advertising business, which was satisfying and defining, until she reached midlife. In search of another adventure, she began her Hourglass Solution by dusting off her Ph.D. and teaching sociology. She is currently a columnist for *InsideOut* Magazine and is a founding partner of Hourglass, Inc. Paula has two grown children and lives with her husband Philip in Hudson, New York, where her journey continues.